English

in perspective

English
in perspective

Felicity Horne

Glenda Heinemann

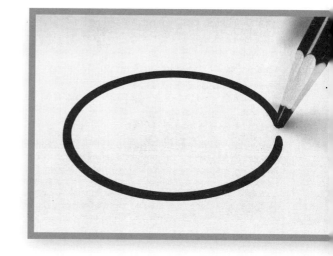

OXFORD

UNIVERSITY PRESS

SOUTHERN AFRICA

OXFORD
UNIVERSITY PRESS
SOUTHERN AFRICA

Oxford University Press Southern Africa (Pty) Ltd

Vasco Boulevard, Goodwood, Cape Town, Republic of South Africa
P O Box 12119, N1 City, 7463, Cape Town, Republic of South Africa

Oxford University Press Southern Africa (Pty) Ltd is a subsidiary of
Oxford University Press, Great Clarendon Street, Oxford OX2 6DP.

The Press, a department of the University of Oxford, furthers the University's objective of
excellence in research, scholarship, and education by publishing worldwide in

Oxford New York

Auckland Cape Town Dar es Salaam Hong Kong Karachi
Kuala Lumpur Madrid Melbourne Mexico City Nairobi
New Delhi Shanghai Taipei Toronto

With offices in

Argentina Austria Brazil Chile Czech Republic France Greece
Guatemala Hungary Italy Japan Poland Portugal Singapore South Korea
Switzerland Turkey Ukraine Vietnam

Oxford is a registered trade mark of Oxford University Press
in the UK and in certain other countries

Published in South Africa
by Oxford University Press Southern Africa (Pty) Ltd, Cape Town

English in perspective
ISBN 978 0 19 578194 6

© Oxford University Press Southern Africa (Pty) Ltd 2006

Publisher: Marian Griffin
Editor: Lorraine Cox
Designer: Mark Standley
Cover design: Brigitte Rouillard and Samantha Rowles
Indexer: Gudrun Kaiser

Set in 11pt on 14pt Minion by RHT desktop publishing cc, Durbanville
Printed and bound by ABC Press, Cape Town

Acknowledgements
The authors and publisher gratefully acknowledge permission to reproduce copyright material
in this book. Every effort has been made to trace copyright holders, but if any copyright
infringements have been made, the publisher would be grateful for information that would
enable any omissions or errors to be corrected in subsequent impressions.

116253

Contents

Preface

The linguist S. I. Hayakawa once said that if fish had to examine their lives scientifically, the last subject they would study is water. Fish are surrounded by water, and depend utterly upon it for life. Yet they do not begin to understand what it is, why they need it, or how it sustains them.

Many of us have the same relation to language that fish have to water. We are so close to it that we often take it completely for granted. Yet it is all around us and pervades and affects every area of our lives. Without language, we could not function properly, nor would we be fully human.

English in perspective aims to provoke students to reflect on this living medium – to become more critically aware of how we use language and how it is used all around us. We want to spotlight some of the problems that language gives rise to in the real world. Although we aim to increase understanding of language issues in general, we focus on the South African language context in particular, and, most specifically, on English in South Africa.

How did this book come into being?

English in perspective is the result of a process that started in 1997 in the English Education Unit (a subsection of the English Department) at the University of South Africa. Ken Saycell, who was then in charge of English teacher education, identified the need for a language studies course in teacher education. He devised the initial framework of such a course, and Glenda Heinemann was contracted to write the study units based on this foundation. Felicity Horne taught and examined the course, and wrote additional tutorial material as she progressed. Initially, the course was designed specifically with teacher trainees in mind, but the scope subsequently widened to include any first-year students of English.

In addition to being given their study material, students who registered for this course were obliged to buy two prescribed books – overseas publications, which became increasingly expensive as the rand devalued. These books were not entirely satisfactory, as they explored linguistic issues in more detail than was required by first year undergraduates. Moreover, they did not cover language issues in the South African context.

It became increasingly apparent that a real need existed for a book on English language studies for South African students at first-year tertiary level. The book had to be affordable, accessible (in terms of content), and particularly relevant to the complex, post-1994 South African language situation. Encouraged by Ken Saycell's successor, Professor Leonie Viljoen, and by Myles Holloway, Felicity submitted a proposal for such a book in 2001. When this was accepted, it became her project to recast the original course material, to integrate selected texts from a wealth of newspaper articles she had collected over time, and add connecting pieces, including activities for students to engage in. The whole was shaped into the present book, which, we are confident, is academic yet readable.

The authors wish to acknowledge the role of Ken Saycell's vision in the genesis of this book. He conceptualized the basic structure that we were able to build on and complete. We would also like to thank our colleagues in the English Education Unit for their support during the writing and editing process. Special appreciation goes to Dr Norah Haussmann, Felicity's ex-colleague and dear friend, for reading the entire manuscript and offering valuable comments based on a lifetime of English teaching experience.

Felicity Horne and Glenda Heinemann

1 Why English?

CHAPTER OUTLINE

In this chapter, we consider the status of the English language in South Africa and in the world. Linguistically, all languages are equal, but some, such as English, currently enjoy greater prestige and power than others, both locally and internationally. We shall be thinking about the reasons for this, and about the implications for the other official languages in South Africa.

LEARNING OUTCOMES

By the end of this chapter you should be able to demonstrate the following knowledge, skills, values, and attitudes:

Knowledge

You should understand
- why all languages are linguistically equal and complex
- the role and status of English as a world language
- the role of English in South Africa
- the role of English versus the other primary South African languages in education, and
- the arguments for and against the dominance of the English language in South Africa.

Skills

You should be able
- to understand and explain conflicting opinions in the debate about the importance of English
- to summarize and contrast given texts in table form, and

- to express your own opinions about the language issues discussed in this chapter.

Values and attitudes

You should develop
- respect for the equality of all languages
- an understanding of the commonly held opinion that proficiency in English is necessary for social and economic advancement, and
- an appreciation of the value of maintaining the primary languages of all South African peoples.

INTRODUCTION

English is only one of eleven languages given official status in the South African Constitution, the others being Sepedi, Sesotho, Setswana, siSwati, Tshivenda, Xitsonga, Afrikaans, isiNdebele, isiXhosa and isiZulu. Officially, all eleven languages enjoy equal status. Thus, in theory, English has no greater status than the other ten languages.

In practice, however, the situation is very different. English is far more widely used than the Constitution would seem to recommend or recognize. Government documents and other official notices usually appear in English only. Parliamentary debate is normally conducted in English.

Why is this the case? Why has the South African government promoted the English language to this position of dominance?

English is favoured over the other official languages because, although it is the mother tongue or primary language (PL) of only 9% of the general South African population, it is the most widely used *additional* language (AL), making it a *lingua franca* (common language) within the country. It was the language chosen for the liberation struggle as the means of uniting the different language groups within that movement, and has now become the language of national unity. In addition, it is also the only one of the eleven languages that is used beyond the borders of South Africa, thus making international and diplomatic communication possible. English is a world language, and being fluent in it has undeniable advantages. These are some of the reasons why it is so highly prized by many people.

However, precisely because it holds this favoured position and is used more than the other official languages, a strong hostility towards the English language exists in some quarters. Many people feel angry and resentful that English usually takes precedence over the other official South African languages. We shall be considering these perceptions and reactions more closely later in the book.

In the South African Constitution it is stated that 'all official languages must enjoy parity of esteem and must be treated equitably' (Section 6 (4) of Act 108 of 1996). In other words, all official languages have equal value and enjoy equal respect. On what basis can one judge the 'value' of a language? In what ways can languages be said to be 'equal'? Let us first look at the *Oxford Advanced Learner's Dictionary* to find the definition of the word 'equal'.

> **equal** *adj*. ... **2** Having the same rights or being treated the same as other (people), without differences such as race, religion or sex being considered. EG *The company has an **equal** opportunities policy* (= gives the same chances of employment to everyone). ... *The desire for a more equal society* (= in which everyone has the same rights and chances).
> *noun* a person or thing with the same quality or with the same status, rights, etc. of another.
> *verb* **1** To be the same in size, quantity, value, etc. as something else.[1]

Do you think equality implies the idea of *deserving* the same treatment? This may be useful when you consider your own opinions about the equality of languages, which is what you should do now.

For the moment, we would like you to set aside the *idea* of the equality of languages. For now, think about ways in which the idea could be demonstrated in *practice*, and write them down. Below are some examples of day-to-day situations in which equality may or should be considered. In your opinion, how should such facts or situations be handled? Once you have answered this question, add some situations of your own to the list.

1   The classroom, in which learners speak a variety of different languages.
2   The current status of certain minority languages in South Africa, such as the Khoisan languages (Bushman and Hottentot languages) and South African Sign Language.
3   The use, or lack of use, of the eleven official languages of South Africa in official contexts, such as government publications and notices.
4   The use of the various official languages and South African Sign Language for television broadcasting.

You could also ask yourself whether *you* have ever been in a situation where you have felt that your primary language has not been treated or regarded as equal to the languages of other people. If so, how did this feel? How would you have liked that situation to be handled?

Remember that your own opinions and thoughts on language issues are valuable. You may wish to have a notebook or journal handy to jot down various points.

We hope that the questions above have suggested to you that *applying* the concept of the equality of languages is less easy than thinking about it in abstract terms. When the equality of languages involves the real-life circumstances of real people (especially when the needs of different language groups have to be balanced with one another) it becomes more complex.

Having looked at the dictionary entry, and at situations in which the equality of languages is an issue, we explore certain perceptions surrounding the *equality of languages*.

ARE SOME LANGUAGES 'BETTER' THAN OTHERS?

Many people believe that certain languages are 'superior' to others. Some people have suggested that certain languages are 'primitive', having a simple grammar and a limited vocabulary. These people believe that speakers of such 'primitive' languages have to use body language and gestures to make up for what the language lacks in words. 'Primitive' languages are thought by some to lack the abstract terms that enable conceptual thinking, thereby making religious belief or intellectual debate impossible.

The modern study of linguistics has shown that such beliefs are mistaken. Investigation of the languages of so-called primitive cultures has established that these languages are fully developed and just as complex as the languages spoken by so-called civilized groups. Of course it is difficult, when comparing languages, to measure complexity in any exact way, because naturally there are linguistic differences, but it is safe to say that all languages have complex grammars and vocabulary to serve the purposes of their speakers fully. It is quite wrong to assume that there are underdeveloped languages which limit the expression of their users and cannot satisfy their needs.

EQUAL, BUT NOT EQUALLY POWERFUL

Let us look again at the *equality of languages.*

While it is true that all languages are equal; that they can express all the needs of their speakers; and that they are all complex in terms of their structure, unfortunately not all languages are able to grant their speakers equal *access* to power and influence.

For centuries, Latin and classical Greek were thought to be superior languages, and models of linguistic excellence, and so were held in higher esteem than living, spoken languages. Latin was the medium of education throughout the Middle Ages. French has been used as a language of international diplomacy up to the present day, which has given it a special status. The term *lingua franca* (Italian for 'Frankish tongue', and meaning any common language used by people with several different primary languages) captures the special status French enjoyed for centuries as a universal medium, linking different nations and language groups. It is a fact that the languages mentioned here once held greater prestige than others, but the basis of this 'superiority' was historical and political, not linguistic.

The view that all languages are equal is based on the important foundation that all languages have developed to express the needs of their users. There is no such thing as a 'primitive' or 'simple' language. All languages have a complex grammar of one kind or another, either in terms of word-endings, or of word-order. All languages are equal in this regard.

We would like to stress that if a certain language was more useful or prestigious than others during a given period in history, this is because the speakers themselves were more powerful at the time, and not because the language itself was or is in any way superior.

Economic or military power and religious influence can also increase the status of a particular language. During the nineteenth century, for example, colonization carried European languages into many different places all over the world, including Africa. English, of course, was one of these languages. Let us briefly consider the historical reasons that have made English the world language it now is.

THE SPREAD OF ENGLISH

The English language has grown in two different ways. First, the language itself has increased in size over the centuries in terms of the sheer extent of its vocabulary. This is mainly because different invaders and conquerors of England (including the Romans, the Vikings, the Danes, and the French) brought masses of new expressions and words into the language. Second, the English language has spread geographically. The numbers of English speakers multiplied when the English-speaking people who colonized foreign populations, brought their English language with them. In these new environments, the local colonizing English-speaking people became 'nativized', absorbing vocabulary and other language features from the indigenous communities they lived among. The English language has thus grown and spread over time, driven by political, economic, historical, and geographical changes.

Changing needs of people throughout history have naturally created changes in language. Today, rapidly developing technology is having a major impact on the development of the English language. Dhamija remarks that new linguistic forms and styles have been released that would have been unthinkable just thirty to forty years ago. He states that 'to meet the challenges of the print and electronic media, English has expanded immensely, both in terms of its coverage and stylistic variation, making it perhaps the most widely used and flexible medium in the world today'.[2]

An outline of the history of the worldwide spread of English follows.

The expansion of the English language over the world began in the seventeenth century, with the first American settlements, but it is in the Later Modern English period (from the eighteenth century onwards) that this expansion has been really spectacular, and that English has become the principal international language. Until about 150 years ago, the major speech-area of the language was still Britain, but in about 1850 the population of the United States overtook that of England, and then shot far ahead, so that North America has become the main centre of the English-speaking community, with some 20-million native-speakers in Canada and over 200-million in the United States. The British Isles remain the second most important area (nearly 58 million), followed by Australia, New Zealand and South Africa. English is also important as a second language in many parts of the world, especially in former British colonial possessions like Nigeria and India.[3]

The tremendous *commercial* power of the United States of America has accelerated the spread of English throughout the world. The pervasive spread of 'American English', together with American values, fashions, habits, and the American lifestyle, have been humorously described as 'coca-colonialism' and 'the Macdonaldization of the world'. In the words of John Pickford:

> English has not become a dominant world language primarily because of its linguistic qualities. It has been spread first by conquest and colonization and subsequently by the cultural and economic power of the Anglo-Saxon countries, especially the United States.[4]

THE SIGNIFICANCE OF THE SPREAD OF ENGLISH

What are the implications of the spread of English as a world language?

English today assumes enormous importance as a world language. When a language spreads widely and comes to be regarded as a world language, this has major implications for those who can speak it, as well as those who cannot. Those who have English as their primary language are automatically at an advantage. They do not have to waste time learning it, and are comfortable using it as a means of communication. On one hand, people who have mastered the world language become more influential in world affairs and scientific research.

On the other hand, those who do not have English as their primary language are at a distinct disadvantage. It takes far more mental or cognitive effort for them to understand ideas expressed in it and to express their own thoughts clearly and accurately. This naturally affects their efficiency and sense of self-esteem, which in turn affects the way they present themselves and their ideas.

A world language gives its speakers and its originating culture an inflated importance and influence. In contrast, minority (non-world) languages suffer, and in some cases have actually become extinct. When the Spanish colonized parts of South America, for example, certain indigenous groups lost their languages. Language is so closely tied up with a sense of national identity that the speakers of minority languages often feel threatened and undervalued when a world language plays a big role in their lives. They feel that their languages and cultures are in danger of dying out. They also feel personally disempowered by not being proficient in the world language.

As a language spreads and is gradually adopted by people with other primary tongues, the additional language undergoes changes. It begins to develop into new spoken varieties. Thus we find different versions of the same root language. As South Africans know, South African English is different from American or Australian English. If varieties of English develop in sufficiently different ways, they could become *mutually unintelligible*. In other words, the situation could arise where a British English speaker cannot understand an American English speaker. George Bernard Shaw summed up such a paradox in a characteristically witty way when he described Britain and America as 'two countries separated by the same language'. But, more recently, improved methods of travel and communication seem to lessen the danger of language varieties growing 'away' from each other and resulting in a loss of mutual intelligibility.

When a language is used globally, as English is, it obviously gains importance and enhanced status. This might be considered advantageous for a language. However, some people feel that, by spreading into different parts of the world and developing into different local varieties, a world language is itself under threat. They fear that a new global variety may emerge with so many distinct new features that it bears little resemblance to the original language or language varieties of only a few years earlier.

English is regarded as a world language for a number or reasons, some of which we list below:

- English is used as an official or semi-official language in over 60 countries
- it is dominant or well-established on all six continents
- it is the main language of books, newspapers, airports and air-traffic control, international business and academic conferences, science, technology, medicine, sport, pop music, and advertising
- three-quarters of all the world's mail is written in English
- of all the information in the world's electronic retrieval systems, 80% is stored in English, and
- English radio programmes are received by over 150 million people in 120 countries.[5]

The list could continue, but the above points should provide enough evidence that English is indeed a world language. Dhamija observes that in view of its spread and use, it may be regarded as the most widely used language in the world. He points out that almost every country in the world communicates with other countries through English. He states that 'English is perhaps the most powerful link language in the world. The shrinking of the globe is due as much to this communicative link as to the communication links provided by supersonic aviation and telecommunication'.[6]

Below is the first of a number of activities in this book. We suggest that you spend a little time thinking about the questions and jotting down your thoughts in a notebook before you attempt to do the activities. This preparation will help you to understand and remember the important points discussed in this book, and will save you time in the long run.

Activity 1 The spread of English

1   What are the factors that contribute to the spread of a language? How have these factors contributed to the spread of English throughout the world?
2   Why would the emergence and spread of a world language not be welcomed by speakers of other languages?
3   In what ways would the spread of English in South Africa be viewed with disapproval by those who are not able to use it?
4   What advantages are enjoyed by those South Africans who do speak English, either as a first (primary) language or as a second (additional) language?
5   Explain why a language may actually be threatened if it becomes a world language.

(You will find our suggested answers to these questions at the end of this book.)

LANGUAGE AS A MEANS OF ACCESS IN SOUTH AFRICA

What is the situation regarding the English language in South Africa? We have seen that all languages are equal, but that some (like English) have spread more widely than others and offer great advantages to those who can use them.

What can be done to enable as many people as possible to gain access to these advantages? From what we have discussed above, it seems as though the ability to speak, read and write English would give people the opportunity to enjoy important benefits. This view seems to be held by many parents of school-going children, who are eager for their children to learn English, no matter what their primary language.

THE ROLE OF ENGLISH VERSUS OTHER PRIMARY LANGUAGES IN EDUCATION

In South Africa, some parents who speak African languages and many parents who speak Afrikaans have chosen to send their children to English-medium schools from as early as the first grade, because they want their children to learn English and to have all their instruction in English from an early age.

Do they feel that the English language is more practical, valuable or worthwhile than their own? If so, for what purpose or purposes is English more valuable? How do you view the opinion that English is more 'valuable' than other primary languages, in the light of what you have learned about the equality of languages? What effect could the decision to send children to English-medium schools have on the non-English primary languages spoken in the home?

Read the following article by Smangaliso Mkhatshwa:

Being multilingual defines being South African

THE CONSTITUTION of the Republic of South Africa recognises that our cultural diversity is a valuable national asset. Hence the need to promote, develop and respect all languages used in our country. Being multilingual should be a defining characteristic of being South African. In this article I want to make a strong plea for the preservation, promotion and development of African languages. Language is not simply a vehicle to transport oral messages, but is a critical part of a people's culture. It is a memory-bank of a people's collective struggles over a period of time. The Kenyan author Ngugi wa Thiong'o shares his profound insight into the role of language in the historical consciousness and development of nations. He says:

> It is this aspect of language, as a collective memory-bank of a given people which has made some people ascribe mystical independence to language. It is the same aspect which has made nations and peoples take up arms to prevent 'total annihilation' or assimilation of their languages, because it is tantamount to annihilating that people's collective memory-bank of past achievements and failures which form the basis of their common identity. It is like uprooting that community from history ...

One's home/mother language is an important cognitive and communication tool. At present I do not believe that we Africans are doing justice to this noble cause of safeguarding our languages. On the contrary, we seem to be doing everything possible to bastardise and downgrade our beautiful languages.

Three months ago I called a friend of mine. His eleven-year-old boy answered the phone. Ngicela ukukhuluma nobaba, mntanami, I said in isiZulu. 'What! What do you say?' screamed the offended child. I heard him consulting the 'helper' (a euphemism for a female domestic servant). The 'helper' apologised and explained that the boy did not speak any Zulu! (Despite the fact that his father's command of the language would have made Shaka or Dingane proud.) The response of the boy's father was typical. He bemoaned the failure of the white-run schools to offer African languages. These experiences reminded me of some uncomfortable home truths. Most middle class blacks speak English to their children at home. They regard their children as clever simply because they speak English without an accent. The result is that these children become culturally alienated because they neither belong to the white Anglo-Saxon world nor to the African culture, which they clearly despise.

This is a classic case of cultural alienation and the consequences of colonisation. Carbon copying things that are English or American including their language may enhance one's chances of acceptability in those societies. The reason is simple. Through language one is socialised into their culture, history and habits ... Failure to communicate in an African language is alienating young urban blacks from their relatives in the rural areas. Language has become an obstacle rather than an opportunity for effective communication.[7]

Activity 2. The value of primary language and culture

Think about the above article, and jot down your answers to the following questions:

1   How does the writer of this passage feel about the fact that children who are alienated from African languages (such as the Zulu child referred to) lose their mother tongue or primary language? Why does the writer feel this way?

2   Do you think the Zulu child has lost something of value, or do you regard him as very lucky to have mastered English at the expense of Zulu?

3   Why do you think some non-English-speaking parents (or parents whose additional language is English) place so much stress on the learning of

English by their children? What are the advantages that such parents might have in mind for their children?

4 Consider the statement that certain parents 'regard their children as clever simply because they speak English without an accent'. Assess the validity of this viewpoint.

5 What does it mean for a child to be 'culturally alienated'?

6 If you think it is important for a child to keep his or her primary language, who do you think should be responsible for this? Is it the parents' responsibility? Is it the school's (as the father in this article appears to believe)? Do you think he is right to blame the school for the fact that his child speaks no Zulu?

7 Does one have to take an 'either/or' stance on this issue? Is it possible to reach a compromise?

(Compare your responses with those we suggest at the end of this book.)

This activity should have stimulated your own thinking on these topical language issues. They are certainly the kinds of questions that you, as a student of language, need to think about.

WHAT THE EXPERTS SAY

From an educational viewpoint, it is believed to be vitally important that a child receives at least the foundation phase of education through the medium of his or her mother tongue or primary language. Concepts and skills should be well established in the PL (primary language) before an AL (additional language) is taught.

Heeding these principles, South African education policy today follows the *additive bilingualism* model, which recommends that children learn an additional language *while maintaining their primary language*. This contrasts with the *subtractive* approach to additional-language teaching in which the child gains an additional language but loses his or her primary language or mother tongue. The latter approach (the results of which were described in the Smangaliso Mkhatshwa article) is believed to be culturally alienating and harmful to the child.

On the importance of primary language proficiency, Michael Morris writes:

Mother-tongue proficiency the bedrock of learning, say experts

THE GENERAL thrust of all international research on language tuition and education is that mother-tongue proficiency is essential to mastering a second language, and to academic success generally. Ironically, many South African parents, acting on a sense that English proficiency is economically and socially desirable, are in favour of practices that risk harming rather than helping their children. Millions of South African children are being disadvantaged by being made to learn English too soon.

Pretoria News, 13 February, 2002 (shortened and adapted)

Several studies have proved that cognitive processes work less efficiently through the additional language. Comprehension tasks take about twice as long in the AL as in the PL, and production tasks (tasks that require the learner to produce creative language through speech or writing) take about three times as long. People are much worse at mental arithmetic in their additional language than in their primary language. In general, the mind is less efficient in an AL whatever it is doing. This is sometimes called the 'cognitive deficit'.[8]

Since competence in English does have huge advantages for the child, English proficiency remains an important goal of teaching. However, the child must continue to develop proficiency in and maintain the primary language, since, as we have seen, this is essential for intellectual growth and academic success. Also, loss of the mother tongue would effectively cut off the child's traditional and cultural roots and destroy the child's sense of identity.

Ngugi wa Thiong'o (quoted by Smangaliso Mkhatshwa earlier) has written feelingly on the damaging effects on the child and the community of which the child forms a part, if indigenous languages are replaced with English. He fully explores the way cultural values are imbibed and instilled while language is being learned. If an African child is educated through English, he or she is subjected to alien cultural values and encouraged to look on Europe as the centre of civilization. Mental processes and values are conditioned in such a way that the child comes to deny his or her original image or identity and loses confidence in his or her linguistic and cultural heritage. Instead of developing the abilities of these children and empowering them, such education makes them feel that their primary language and culture are inadequate (according to certain Western precepts and 'standards'), and the cruel process of alienation is brought about. In his own words:

> Language carries culture, and culture carries, particularly through orature and literature, the entire body of values by which we come to perceive ourselves and our place in the world .... Language is thus inseparable from ourselves as a community of human beings with a specific form and character, a specific history, a specific relationship to the world.[9]

From this point of view, the learning of English too soon and at the expense of other primary languages could have the effect of *dis*empowering the individual.

THE DOMINANCE OF ENGLISH

As we have discussed, English is more widely used in South Africa than are the other official languages. Naturally, this fact is often resented: witness the following editorial in the *Pretoria News*:

Time to turn talk into action

THE PEOPLES of the world celebrated International Mother Tongue Day last Thursday, February 21 2002. The beauty and diversity of the languages of the world, and by extension the richness of different cultures, was also marked locally by MPs, who took part in special debates and a lunch.

But the day's significance was lost on most of us. Even the MPs' celebration was somewhat farcical, considering that English still dominates in spite of the fact that 90% of MPs have a mother tongue other than English. Tellingly, an ANC MP was hampered from speaking in

Setswana because of problems with the translation service. Clearly, as IFP MP Farouk Cassim said, English is "moving like a bulldozer over other languages", much to the chagrin of the Afrikaans, Nguni, Sesotho, Shangaan and Venda language groups.

In most instances, the children of these marginalised people are force-fed English as a medium of instruction before they can even master their own languages. This despite the United Nations and experts recommending that children be taught in their mother tongue up to at least Standard 2 or Grade 4. Otherwise, they say, such children ulti-mately struggle with content subjects in later years.

Needless to say, the elevation of English and marginalisation of the country's 10 other official languages is discriminatory, unjust and con-trary to the spirit and letter of the Constitution. Already, the murmurs of protest at this injustice are getting louder by the day. Something must be done before their disaffection turns into something ugly.

Pretoria News, 26 February 2002

Consider the way English is presented in this editorial.
- How is it being portrayed? Try to pinpoint particular examples.
- To what extent are these expressions emotive, and what is the effect of the expressions?
- What is the purpose of this editorial?

You will probably agree that the tone of this editorial is strongly emotive and presents English in a very negative light. The use of powerful images of 'English moving like a bulldozer over other languages', and children being 'force-fed' English at school, portray English as a threatening, destructive force. The purpose of the text is to urge vigorous resistance to the dominance of the English language.

Compare this view with that expressed in an earlier editorial in the same newspaper:

Another English invasion

THE ADVENT of high-speed, hi-tech global communications in business, politics and economics has led to the dominance of English as the language of choice in most spheres of inter-continental communication. This was not a choice forced upon others by Anglo-oriented countries, but instead was brought about by the advancement of technology; English-speaking countries dominated the technology, others adapted to fit in.

This is a sad fact and should be accepted by those South Africans who have lately been griping that the other 10 official languages recognised under our Constitution as having equal status have been down-graded, and that English here too has been chosen as the "official" communications medium by both government and business. South Africa is fast becoming a major global player and is simply following a world-wide trend. It does not mean that the other 10 languages will not survive, nor that they are playing second fiddle to English.

Pretoria News, 13 November, 2001

How does the opinion of the role of English in South Africa in the second editorial ('Another English Invasion') differ from that expressed in the one quoted previously ('Time to turn talk into action')? We have said that this editorial urged resistance to the dominance of English. In contrast:

- What is the purpose of 'Another English invasion'?
- What kind of attitude does the speaker feel we should hold towards English?

Activity 3 Comparison of editorials

1 Try now to summarize the contrasting points of view expressed in the two editorials by means of a table. In the framework below, fill the empty boxes with appropriate comment.

Editorial 1: **Time to turn talk into action**	Editorial 2: **Another English Invasion**
English marginalizes, dominates and will destroy other languages.	Other languages are not threatened by English and will survive.
	The dominance of English has occurred naturally through technological advancement.
	(Implied) Everyone will need English, so it is to the advantage of all children to master it.
The supremacy of English is discriminatory, unjust, and goes against the South African Constitution.	
	We must accept the dominance of the English language.

(Compare your answer with the one we suggest at the end of the book.)

Weighing up these two viewpoints, how do *you* feel about this issue? Do you see English as:

- a destructive force that should be combatted?
- a necessary evil?
- a highly desirable tool?
- or are there elements of more than one of these three options in your response?

If there are elements of more than one of them in your response, you are in good company. William Branford sums up the somewhat contradictory role and perceptions of the English language in South Africa in the following points:

---

1 First and foremost, English provides access to educational and job opportunities.
2 But it acts simultaneously as a barrier to such opportunities for those who lack it, or whose English is poor.
3 It acts integratively as a 'language of wider communication' for people of different mother tongues.
4 But it acts divisively, or may do, between the members of English-speaking elites and those of less fortunate groups with little English, the 'wrong' kind, or none.
5 It is an important key to knowledge, science and world literature and current affairs.
6 But it has been accused of suppressing indigenous traditions and patterns of culture.
7 English and its varieties in South Africa have, furthermore, an identificatory or 'demarcating' role. Through the selection of one language over another, or of one variety of the same language over another, speakers display 'acts of identity'. For South African speakers of English as L2 (AL), important signals of identity are often made by the 'pull' of their L1 (PL) upon their English.[10]

SUMMARY

Here is a summary of the main points discussed in this chapter:
- English is only one of eleven official languages in South Africa, but in practice English is the most widely used. There are important reasons for this.
- All languages are equal. All languages are complex.
- However, some languages are more useful and powerful than others for certain purposes at certain times and in certain situations.
- English has become a world language as a result of historical, geographical, political, economic, and technological factors. This fact has positive and negative implications.

- Because English is used more frequently than the other official South African languages, and because it is a world language, it has acquired an added status in South Africa.
- The dominance of the English language in South Africa arouses strong reactions, many of them negative.
- Opinions regarding the role of English as a medium of instruction vary widely. Some educational experts advise instruction in the primary language for the first few years of schooling, at least. Others recommend the use of the primary language as a medium of instruction even into the high-school phase. The Government endorses the additive-bilingualism model.
- Contradictory viewpoints exist as to whether or not a command of English brings benefits to the individual and the country.

GLOSSARY

Below is a list of some of the main terms relating to language concepts introduced in this chapter, together with brief explanations. You may wish to add some terms of your own.

world language	a particular language that has spread widely and is used all over the world as a *lingua franca*
lingua franca	a common language, or a language which is used to link people who have different primary or mother tongues
status	the standing or position of one language in relation to others; the degree of respect with which the language is viewed
mutually unintelligible	a language may exist in such different varieties that the speakers of different varieties are unable to understand one another
language as a means of access	to use a particular language in order to gain entrance to certain facilities, making the speaker eligible for social and economic opportunities

cultural alienation	becoming estranged or cut off from the cultural community into which you were born
cognitive deficit	limitations on mental efficiency required to process information in an additional language
additive bilingualism	an approach to language teaching where an additional language is taught but the primary tongue is maintained and developed
subtractive language teaching	an approach to language teaching in which an additional language is taught and becomes the 'primary language', replacing the mother tongue, which is lost altogether

ENDNOTES

1 FOX, GWYNETH, ed. 1994. *Essential English Dictionary*. London: Harper Collins Publishers.

2 DHAMIJA, P.V. 1994. 'English as a multiform medium', in Mike Hayhoe and Stephen Parker, *Who owns English?* p. 67. Buckingham: Open University Press.

3 BARBER, C. 1975. 'The later history of English', p. 330, in W. F. Bolton (ed.) *The English language*, p. 330 (extract slightly adapted). London: Sphere Books.

4 PICKFORD, JOHN. 1995. 'Time to cheerfully split the infinitive', in *BBC worldwide*, p. 19, No. 33, July. Quoted in: 1998 Study Guide 1 for the Advanced Certificate in Education, p. 48, compiled by members of the ACE team. Pretoria: University of South Africa.

5 CRYSTAL, DAVID. 1987. *The Cambridge Encyclopedia of Language*, p. 358. Cambridge: Cambridge University Press.

6 DHAMIJA, P.V. 1994. 'English as a multiform medium', in Mike Hayhoe and Stephen Parker, *Who owns English?* p. 62. Buckingham: Open University Press.

7 SMANGALISO MKHATSHWA. 1999. 'Being multilingual defines being South African' in *Pansalb News*, April – June. Pretoria: Pan South African Language Board.

8 COOK, V. 1991. *Second language learning and language teaching*, pp. 52–3. London: Edward Arnold.

9 NGUGI WA THIONG'O. 1986. *Decolonising the mind: the politics of language in African literature*, p. 16. London: James Curry.

10 BRANFORD, WILLIAM. 1996. Adaptation of 'English in South African society: a preliminary overview', in Vivian de Klerk (ed.) *Focus on South Africa*, p. 36. Amsterdam: John Benjamins.

2 Which English?

So far, we have indicated that many varieties of one language can and do exist. There are many different varieties of English spoken in the world, and indeed in South Africa. This chapter explores some language varieties and how they are perceived and used.

LEARNING OUTCOMES

By the end of this chapter you should be able to demonstrate the following knowledge, skills, values, and attitudes:

Knowledge

You should understand
- that many different varieties of English exist
- what is meant by the 'standard' variety of a language
- the position of standard English in South Africa
- that all languages are subject to change
- that attitudes towards language use may be prescriptive or descriptive, and
- that the standard form of a language helps all people who use the language to understand one another.

Skills

You should be able
- to recognize non-standard features of English
- to distinguish between a prescriptive and a descriptive approach to language use, and
- to apply each of these approaches to a text.

Values and attitudes

You should develop
- respect and tolerance for linguistic diversity, and
- objectivity in describing the facts of language use, while acknowledging the equality of all languages.

LANGUAGE VARIETY

Not all people who speak a language speak it in the same way. The term *variety* is used to describe these differences. A variety of a particular language is one of the *forms* it takes, depending on the circumstances in which the language is being used, and the reason for its use. A language may be changed by the people who are using it, according to who and where they are, and what they are doing.

This is true of English, as of other languages. The particular variety of English that is chosen in a given situation may depend on, among other things, *geographical*, *cultural*, *social* or *situational* factors (the latter could include the degree of formality required in the communicative situation).

Two major factors that influence language variety are *space* and *time*. 'Space' in this context refers to *regional* or *geographical* differences. In the case of English, there is an obvious difference between the English spoken by someone from America and that spoken by someone from England. 'Time' refers to *historical changes* that have taken place in a language: think of the difference between modern English and the language of Shakespeare, for example.

RECOGNIZING DIFFERENT VARIETIES

What exactly are the differences between language varieties? What kinds of differences are there, and where can these varieties be found?

The differences may be *phonological*, *lexical* or *grammatical*. In other words, different varieties may *sound* different (phonological); they may use different *words* (lexical); or they may use different *sentence structures* (grammatical).

VARIETIES OF ENGLISH

Let us look at regional or geographical varieties of English first. Within the British Isles, English is spoken in England, Wales, Scotland, Northern Ireland and the Republic of Ireland. (Other languages are also spoken in some of these countries, but we are not going to discuss these languages here.)

There are definite differences between the varieties of English spoken in these countries. However, there are also differences between the varieties of English spoken *within* the various countries. In England, for example, the English spoken in Yorkshire is different from that spoken in London. In Scotland, people living in Glasgow speak differently from those living a short distance away in Aberdeen.

These local dialects of English are not our main concern here, however. We are more concerned with the situation of the English language as a *global* or world language.

Figure 2.1 A map of the British Isles[1]

Dialect and accent

Many people use the term *dialect* to refer to a language variety. What does this term mean? Does it simply refer to the fact that different groups of people speak English with different accents? What do we mean when we say that people 'speak with an accent' or that they 'use a certain dialect'? Is there a difference between *accent* and *dialect*?

Accent refers to a particular kind of pronunciation, the way particular words are sounded. English, for example, is spoken in different parts of the world with a variety of accents.

Dialect, on the other hand, involves not only pronunciation but differences in vocabulary and grammar as well.

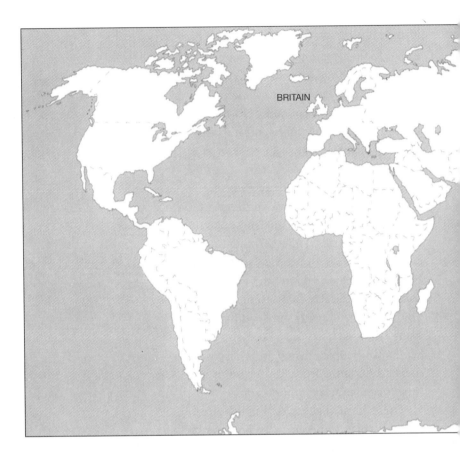

In Chapter 1 we pointed out that English has spread to many countries in the world. It is now used as an official language in countries such as England, Scotland, Wales, Northern Ireland, the Republic of Ireland, the United States of America, Canada, Australia, New Zealand, South Africa, India, Nigeria, Zimbabwe, and Zambia.

These countries are separated from one another by great distances and, until relatively recently, communication between them was slow. As we mentioned above, languages change over time. The changes that have occurred in one place are very often different from the ones that have taken place elsewhere. As a result, the English spoken in one area differs from the English spoken in other areas, and all of these varieties are different from the English spoken in England itself.

Some people still think that the English spoken in England is the only 'correct' English, because that is where the language originated. What is your opinion?

Figure 2.2 A map of the world, showing the position and size of the British Isles[2]

WHICH VARIETY OF ENGLISH IS THE 'RIGHT' ONE TO USE?

There is no single, simple answer to this question. As we mentioned above, *situation* determines to a large extent which variety of English will be used. Different varieties of English are appropriate in different situations.

STANDARD ENGLISH

Although different varieties of English (like different languages) are equal in their complexity; equal in linguistic terms; and serve the needs of the speakers that use them, they are not equal in status. *Standard English* enjoys the greatest prestige, but what do we mean by 'standard' English?

Standard English developed from the variety spoken in the area around London in the sixteenth century. This variety gained prestige, mainly because it was the variety spoken at Court (in other words, by royalty and by the courtiers, or those closely associated with royalty).

In modern times, standard English is the variety taught at school and is used for official purposes. It is the kind of English used by the news-readers and presenters on radio and television. The standard form refers to a fairly formal variety, and is most common in its written form. Standard English is used as a means of communication that links many peoples and countries of the world.

Non-standard forms of English, in contrast, include all the other varieties of English, such as local vernacular forms; dialects that have lexical, grammatical and phonological deviations from standard English; and informal varieties that might include colloquialisms and slang.

There are definite social implications of being able or unable to use standard English. Standard English is often associated with personal prestige. Competency in standard English can provide entry to the gate-way of economic opportunity and higher education, among other things. Lack of competency in standard English can often block the way. Being able to speak and write standard English is a very useful and necessary skill if we wish to prosper in the wider world.

SOUTH AFRICAN VARIETIES OF ENGLISH

Varieties of South African English have been shaped by various factors. Major factors are the influences on the language by the various popu-lation groups using it, which has led to the emergence of different South African varieties of English. Roughly speaking, five population groups can be identified: Afrikaans speakers of European descent, English and Afrikaans speakers of mixed or 'Coloured' descent, speakers of indige-nous languages of African descent, Indians of Indian and African descent, and English speakers of European descent.

The formation of these population groups and their varieties of spoken English took place under the former apartheid regime. We cannot ignore the radical effects of the old political dispensation on the formation of different language varieties in South Africa. Indeed, our turbulent political history has played a crucial role in shaping them.

As Silva notes:

> The effects of apartheid ... the separation of communities into socially distinct groups, and the powerful consciousness of ethnic divergence which developed, impacted upon all aspects of life, including language. White, Black, Coloured, and Indian South Africans all use English, with varying degrees of sophistication, but as a result of their isolation from one another, native English, Afrikaans English, Black English, Coloured English, and Indian English are distinguishable from one another, each containing lexical items unknown to people of other groups, and each exhibiting characteristic pronunciations and even grammatical structures.[3]

This is not to suggest that the different population groups are well defined or homogenous. Nevertheless, it cannot be denied that there are distinguishing features in each kind of English spoken within each loosely structured group.

There are also other different English dialects used by members of particular South African subcultures who use their own variety of English as a badge of identity. More will be said about these dialects in Chapter 5.

ATTITUDES TOWARDS LANGUAGE USAGE

'Listen to this idiot! How can they get people like this to speak on television?'

'Why can't they speak English properly!'

'His accent was shocking! Just another example of the way standards are dropping everywhere!'

- Have you heard this kind of remark in response to the way some people speak English in South Africa today?
- What does it mean to 'speak English properly'?
- What sort of person makes these judgements?
- On what criteria are these judgements based?
- What emotions lie behind them?
- What do they illustrate about people's attitudes?
- Are these attitudes legitimate?

Such comments and judgements about the use of everyday English are often heard. They are generally voiced with real indignation by individuals who speak as though they are authorities on language matters. Yet this is usually far from the case. People are, of course, entitled to pass opinions, but their opinions should be informed.

- Why do people become so heated about language issues?
- Where do these judgemental attitudes come from?

THE PRESCRIPTIVE TRADITION

In South Africa, many of us have been through a school system that made us feel as though the way we speak English is not 'right'. We have been told not to use slang, to pronounce our words differently to the way we pronounce words at home, and to be careful about our grammar, which was often judged to be 'faulty'. As a result, we often feel nervous about our own use of the English language, and find ourselves listening critically for other people's 'mistakes'.

Though most of you are not experts on language, all of you probably had strong *opinions* and *beliefs* about language even before you began reading this book. These opinions and beliefs have been formed by your experience, education, social conditioning and development, including the way your teachers made you feel about the way you spoke and wrote.

David Crystal remarks that:

> [t]he English language has suffered badly at the hands of the grammarians over the centuries. Many people have left school with the impression that English grammar is a dull, boring, pointless subject … or that they don't know the correct grammar. They feel insecure and defensive. Something is wrong when this happens.[4]

'Experts' such as teachers and editors, who cite authoritative texts such as dictionaries and grammar books, often work from the premise that there are 'right' and 'wrong' ways of using language. Such assumptions, even when they are referred to as 'conventions', fail to take account of the fact that there is not only one variety of written language to be used, but different varieties of the same language, just as there are different varieties of spoken language. The choice of which variety is the 'best' depends on the circumstances in which the language is being used, and why.

Rules of correct usage relate chiefly to the *standard* variety of English, the variety that is most often written. However, teachers and other 'authorities' do not always recognize that written and spoken language are *different varieties*, even when used by the same person. We will discuss the differences between written and spoken English in much greater detail in Chapter 6, but the point must be made here that it is misguided to judge *speech* by the standards of *written* language.

There is also a failure to recognize that what is unacceptable usage in one context may be completely suitable in another. Slang or swearing may be out of place in a classroom discussion or university conference, but may be normal in an informal conversation among friends. Particular dialects using non-standard English forms have their place in certain contexts as well.

Different accents and pronunciations used in the media often arouse a great deal of annoyance. This has been particularly evident since 1994, now that additional-language English speakers are heard much more often on radio and television. Those people accustomed to hearing 'BBC accents' (British Broadcasting Corporation), or the British 'received pronunciation', often object to what they believe to be 'badly spoken' English. 'Badly spoken English' in this context is likely to refer to the accent of a newsreader or presenter whose English is an additional and not a primary language. Such beliefs ignore the reality that South African English cannot be 'BBC English'. It is inevitable that there are local forms of South African English, and that different language communities will speak in distinctive ways. There is no harm in this: it is part of what makes our language landscape so colourful.

- Are we implying that anyone can speak English in any way they like?
- Is there no need for English to be taught?
- Is the notion of 'standard' English out of date?

Not so. Standard English, although only one variety of several in South Africa, does have a particularly important status, and it has this for good reasons. In this chapter we shall be considering these reasons. We shall also be examining existing attitudes towards language issues in the hope of bringing about greater understanding and tolerance towards a use of language that may differ from our own. We need to get away from the rigid idea that anything that deviates from 'standard' English is necessarily 'bad'.

Consider the viewpoint expressed in the following letter to the editor:

Speak English correctly

A WHILE BACK I saw an item about the girl who had to write an essay given to her by a new teacher. She asked her mother why they got such a boring subject as 'beds' to write about.

Her mother soothed her and told her to try anyway. In receiving her essay back she discovered that the subject was in fact 'birds'.

The other night I was listening to an eminent educator talking about school reform when I was surprised to learn that under the old regime, pupils (sorry – it's learners now) were 'bitten' when they did not do their work. While still wondering where they were bitten, (on their ears, on their hands, on their buttocks?) it dawned on me ... 'beaten'.

Will it not be a cure if at home, we shut down the TV with its bad American and Australian English and rather join a library? Or buy the newspaper? As it is now, these words become a shibboleth for the listener. If English is the common way to understand one another in this country, then surely it should be spoken clearly and correctly.

T B van der Merwe, Waterkloof Ridge
Pretoria News, 26 March, 2001

The writer of this letter takes exception to the pronunciation of certain words. He or she blames Australian and American television programmes for providing 'incorrect' models of speech. The explanation, however, lies closer to home. In certain African languages, there are fewer vowel sounds than there are in English, which easily explains the similar pronunciation of words like 'ship' and 'sheep'. The writer appears to be poorly informed on linguistic matters, yet this does not stop him or her from expressing a strong opinion in an authoritative way. He or she makes no attempt to define what it means to speak English 'correctly', assuming that he or she and we know and agree on the matter. There is no doubt in the writer's mind as to what is 'right' and 'wrong' in this situation.

We all (to a greater or lesser degree) feel that we are the custodians of our own language or variety/varieties of language/languages. This often makes our own attitudes towards language <u>emotional</u> and thus as irrational as the attitude of this writer.

Yet the writer identifies a real problem: there is indeed a genuine misunderstanding because one word is taken for another and this leads to a breakdown in communication. Communication, after all, is one of the chief functions of language. If communication fails, something is definitely wrong and it needs to be addressed. What aspect of English usage has led to the misunderstanding?

Broadly speaking, language can be considered to have three branches:

1 **Lexis** (vocabulary)
2 **Syntax** (sentence structure or grammar)
3 **Phonology** (the sound system, embracing accent and pronunciation)

1 **Lexemes** are items of vocabulary, the building blocks of language. In this case, the word 'bird' is confused with the word 'bed', but not in the speaker's mind. The speaker is thinking of the right concept, but the listener is hearing something different. So this is not a lexical problem. An example of a lexical problem is using the word 'quiet' instead of 'quite' in: 'She was quiet a pretty girl'.

2 **Syntax** involves grammar and the way words are arranged in sentences.
   Examples of syntactical problems are:
   'There *is* too many people in this room' instead of:
   'There *are* too many people in this room'.
   or
   'If I have the books, I *can be able to pass*' instead of:
   'If I have the books, I *will be able to pass*', or
   'If I have the books, I *can pass*'.

3 **Phonology** involves the way language *sounds*. We have already mentioned accent, and the other aspect of phonology is pronunciation. It is tricky to be prescriptive about accent and pronunciation because these vary widely and it is not clear cut what could be considered 'right' or 'wrong', but there are certain problems that could be called 'errors of pronunciation', when syllables of words are wrongly emphasized. One example is the word 'circumstances' which

should have the stress on the first syllable: '*CIR*cumstances'. Often we hear English additional-language speakers talking of 'cir*CUM*-stances', with the stress falling on the second syllable.

Which of these three aspects of language, lexis, syntax or phonology, is involved in the problem of the 'beds' and 'birds' cited in the letter of complaint?

Clearly, it is *phonology* that is giving trouble here. A particular accent (resulting from the fact that the teacher's first language is an indigenous language) has prevented the teacher's speech from being intelligible to the learner, who apparently comes from a different language background.

On a humorous note, a similar misunderstanding (caused by a phonological problem) arose when an advertiser telephoned a Johannesburg newspaper to place an advertisement in the newspaper's classified section. The following information was printed in error:

> Villa for sale. Four bedrooms, two garages, swimming-pool and seven squatters.[5]

What was heard and transcribed was 'seven squatters', but what was intended was 'servants' quarters'.

Mutual intelligibility often breaks down as a result of a lack of understanding of a particular accent or accents. Trying to achieve mutual intelligibility is one of the most important reasons for teaching the standard variety of English. However, learning the standard variety is no guarantee that there will be mutual intelligibility, since one may speak standard English using a variety of accents. Quirk writes:

> There is the myth, for example, that standard English entails a particular accent, 'talking posh'. It does not. Only a trifling minority of standard English speakers have any such accent and standard English is spoken equally well by Bill Clinton, Paul Keating, Virginia Bottomley and John Smith, not to mention Nelson Mandela and F. W. de Klerk.[6]

Phonology is known to be the most difficult aspect of language to regulate and change. Many English additional-language speakers who have mastered English grammar and learned the vocabulary of English so that they speak it fluently and with a high degree of proficiency, never completely 'lose' the accent of their primary or mother tongue.

Before reading any further, pause for a moment to consider your own position in relation to the following statements. Do you hold any particular opinions about language or about particular languages?

Think about the questions below:

- Do you think radio and television journalists in South Africa generally use the English language in a satisfactory manner?
- Do you think the languages taught and used at school should be only of the standard variety? Do you understand exactly what is meant by 'the standard variety'?
- Where and at what stage in your life did you begin to think about the questions above? At school? After school, in discussions with colleagues?

Most of us are likely to have opinions about language issues. You may find that many of your answers to the above questions differ from those provided by other people, which might indicate that such answers are probably expressions of *opinion*, not fact.

This diversity of opinion is not a problem, however. Instead, this diversity provides a 'point of departure' for the study of language. You all start at the same place and have something in common: the fact that you have already formed opinions and beliefs about the use of language. These opinions can form the basis of discussion.

If this is the case, what approach can be taken to the study of language, since opinions and beliefs differ so widely? What is involved in such a study?

Our goal is to make you better informed about language. Instead of dismissing or condemning English that is non-standard or different from your own, you will understand why and how it is different. You will also have a better understanding of standard English and why it is necessary for us all to be able to use it.

Our aim in this book is to provide and discuss information about language that will allow you to participate knowledgeably in activities and debates involving language, in a progressive way that will further the ideals of respect and tolerance.

The scientific method employed in studying information about language involves a detailed and systematic analysis of the available facts.

LANGUAGE, AN EMOTIVE SUBJECT

Language can be a very emotive subject. People judge others by the way they speak. As we have seen, people are often accorded, or denied, respect on the basis of how they use language. This is a hard fact of life whether we agree with it or not. This fact has important implications for day-to-day living. You may find it helpful to jot down answers to the questions below, which are related to the judging of people on the grounds of how they speak and what language they use.

- Consider the point that linguistic factors influence our judgements of personality, intelligence, social status, educational standards, job aptitude, and many other areas of identity and social survival. Can you recall any actual situations that illustrate this statement? Do you think that some people's job prospects are limited by their shortage of skills in one or more of the languages of the country, for example? Are certain people admired because of their abilities in certain languages? Can you think of specific examples?

- Which aspects of language or language varieties do you think are most important in determining attitudes? Is it *which* language is spoken, or *how* it is spoken? If the latter, is it vocabulary, sentence structure, or accent (or all three) that cause the listener to react in certain ways?

- Try to discuss these questions with family members, teachers whom you know, or with anyone else. Ask them to think about the ways in which language factors have influenced their lives and job opportunities.

More about the prescriptive approach

With regard to how the English language is viewed, we are now going to attempt a full explanation of the adjective 'prescriptive'. You will see that the prescriptive approach takes a very *judgemental* stance towards the use of language.

Read the poem by Sipho Sepamla printed below, and answer the questions that follow:

Da same, da same

I doesn't care of you black
I doesn't care of you white
I doesn't care of you India
I doesn't care of you clearlink
if sometimes you Saus Afrika
you gotta big terrible, terrible
somewheres in yourselves

I mean for sure now
all da peoples is make like God
an' da God I knows for sure
He make avarybudy wi' one heart
for sure now dis heart go-go da same
dats for meaning to say
one man no diflent to anader

so now
you see a big terrible terrible stand here
how one man make anader man feel
da pain he doesn't feel hisself
for sure now dats da whole point

sometime you wanna know
how I meaning for is simple
when da nail of say da t'orn tree
scratch little bit little bit of da skin

I doesn't care of say black
I doesn't care of say white
I doesn't care of say India
I doesn't care of say clearlink
I mean for sure da skin
only one t'ing come for sure
an' da one t'ing for sure is red blood
dats for sure da same, da same for avarybudy

so for sure now
you doesn't look anader man in de eye

The prescriptive approach

A *prescriptive* approach to language is based on a concern with the *rules* that govern language usage, and the belief that these rules should be imposed on everyone. The prescriptive point of view assumes that there are 'right' and 'wrong' ways of using language. The prescriptive approach is associated with a rigid, authoritarian attitude. Implicit in this attitude is the belief that certain varieties of language, notably standard English, are 'superior' to others. Non-standard varieties of English are not tolerated and are dismissed as 'ungrammatical'. Non-standard varieties are regarded as 'bad language'.

Activity 1 Poetry and dialect

1 What is unusual about the use of language in this poem? Try to pinpoint some specific examples of unusual usage. How would you describe these? Would you call them 'mistakes' or 'non-standard features'?

2 Would this poem be equally well understood by people from all over the world? What role would geographical or regional factors play here?

3 For English speakers in other parts of the world to understand this poem, what changes would you need to make? Try to rewrite the first stanza of the poem, in more regular, standard English.

4 When written in standard English, does the poem have the same impact?

(Compare your answers with those provided at the end of this book.)

Earlier in this chapter, we asked you to think about the way in which television and radio journalists use English. We asked you to consider whether you thought their use of English is *satisfactory*. On what basis can this question be asked or answered? Who is to decide what is 'satisfactory'?

A shortened extract below, by Robert Kirby, is from a column that appeared in the *Friday* supplement of the *Mail & Guardian* newspaper for the week 15 to 21 October, 1999. Consider the opinions expressed in it.

SABC dumbing up

'*The petrol price has gone up with 60c since the beginning of the year. If it will reach the R3 mark at the end of the year...*' intones SABC television news reporter Joanne Roodt.

'*One of eight people accused are being charged,*' whines Nadia Levin from deep inside the tornado-chic of her latest hairstyle. Close on her heels is an SABC field reporter who tells of someone's assets having been '*fourfeeted*'. This is hastily corrected and in the next bulletin someone else's assets have been '*confisticated*'. Here's another elegant lode: '*The persons found in the possession of the drugs can be full prosecuted.*'

Your first reaction to a grammatical mess like this is often anger. But, minute by minute, as the examples rack up in the average SABC news bulletin, the emotion gradually shifts through embarrassment and pity, and ends up 180° from where it began. At this stage you remember Mr Byron's helpful comment: 'And if I laugh at any mortal thing, 'tis that I may not weep.'

What is quite clear is that the SABC no longer comprehends the scope of its influence on language. Somewhere along the bucking 'transformation' line the corporation shook itself free of its obligations in this wise. There has to be some reason for the persistent use of gutter English in SABC news bulletins, if not a calculated decision. Perhaps the SABC board has elected to ignore linguistic standards in favour of making everything a lot less stressful for the semi-literates who nowadays write the SABC English news and the sub-literates who report it.

Mail & Guardian, 15–21 October, 1999

The writer expresses strong opinions in strong terms. His tone is highly critical; his attitude judgemental. This is an example of a *prescriptive* stance. Do these comments sound familiar? Do you know other people who say things like that? Have you made similar remarks yourself? Let us look again at what such comments imply.

The prescriptive view of language is based on the assumption that one of the varieties of a language is inherently 'better' or more valuable than the others. This preferred variety is usually the 'standard' written variety.

As soon as there is a 'standard' with which other varieties can be compared and against which they can be judged, the notion of *correctness* arises. This notion of correctness underlies the prescriptive approach to language, and is accompanied by *value judgements* about certain forms of usage, such as is evident in the comments above. People who make such comments judge the language of the television and radio journalists against their idea of the 'best' language.

Since one of the many varieties of a particular language is considered more *valuable* than the others, it follows that this variety has a higher *status* than the others. (The word 'status' refers to the *position* of something or someone in relation to others.) Certain varieties of one language can have higher status than others in certain situations.

Do you think that the status of a language variety 'rubs off' on the people who use it? In other words, do people think less of you if you use a variety that may not be considered the 'best' or 'standard' variety?

If they *do* think less of you, is their opinion important to you? Why? Or why not? What influence could their opinion have on your life or your employment prospects? If the way you use language prevents you from getting the job you want, you may be a 'victim' of the prescriptive approach to language.

Conversely, if you think less of people who use a non-standard variety of English, you may want to consider whether or not you also have a prescriptive approach to language.

There is another way of looking at language, however.

THE DESCRIPTIVE APPROACH

An alternative approach to language study or assessment is the *descriptive* approach. What does this approach entail?

A *descriptive* approach to language is concerned with describing *actual* language usage without making judgements about what is 'right' or 'wrong', 'good' or 'bad'. It is associated with a more flexible, open-minded outlook. The descriptive point of view is concerned with what is spoken, not what *should* be spoken. Non-standard varieties of language are considered just as worthy of interest and study as are standard ones.

We have summarized these two views of language in the table below so as to highlight the contrasts between them:

The descriptive approach	The prescriptive approach
concerned with facts of usage	concerned with 'standards'
seeks to describe and record the facts of language diversity	seeks to judge and evaluate usage in terms of rules. Usages are considered 'educated', or banned as 'uneducated'
uses the language itself as its point of reference	uses 'rules' of grammar, legislation and authoritative texts as points of reference

The table in which we contrast the descriptive and prescriptive views may give the impression that there can never be any agreement at all between these views, and between the people who hold them. This certainly has been the case and still is in certain quarters. It seems as though people who hold one view simply cannot understand those who hold the opposite view.

Crystal suggests that these two views described above have even been given _political_ meaning. The prescriptive view has come to be associated with conservatism.[7]

Think about the situation in our own country at the moment. Some people talk a lot about 'standards' and the dangers of 'lowering' or 'dropping' them. Do you think such people are likely to be generally quite conservative? ('Conservative' means wanting to keep things as they are.)

In contrast, the descriptive approach is sometimes associated with a politically progressive position. Again, this may be true of our own local situation. Some people are more concerned with providing opportunities for learners to express themselves in communicative situations, and building their self-esteem, than with getting them to learn the 'rules' of 'correctness' first. Do you think such people are likely to be progressive in the political sense? ('Progressive' means wanting to reform and improve social conditions.)

However, it is not necessary to see these two views as being _opposed_ in this way. Such opposition is based on stereotyped thinking. It is possible to see that the two approaches have much in common, since both are concerned with acceptability, ambiguity, and intelligibility of language.

Activity 2 Viewpoint underlying letter to the editor

Turn back now to the letter to the editor from T B van der Merwe, reproduced on page 32 and decide whether the views expressed there reflect a _prescriptive_ or _descriptive_ approach to English. Justify your answer with close reference to the text.

(Compare your answer with the one provided at the end of this book.)

Activity 3 Prescriptive viewpoint of a newspaper column

We have established that Robert Kirby's response to language usage ('SABC dumbing up') is informed by a prescriptive approach. Refer to his article again. Consider each of the examples he gives:

'The petrol price has gone up with 60 cents …'

'If it will reach the R3 mark …'

'One of eight people are being charged …'

'… fourfeeted …'

'…confisticated…'

'The persons found in the possession of the drugs …'

'… can be full prosecuted…'

How would you correct the examples quoted above that he finds objectionable?

(Compare your answers with the ones provided at the end of this book.)

Activity 4 Applying prescriptive and descriptive approaches

Refer again to the poem 'Da same, da same'. Comment on the language used in this poem from:

1 a prescriptive point of view
2 a descriptive point of view.

(Poets do, of course, have the right to express feelings in whichever way they like. They mould English in different ways to achieve particular effects. This is known as 'poetic licence', and is one of the joys of poetic creativity. Poetry should never be subjected to prescriptive analysis as, for example, a government document might be. So, what we ask you to do here is rather artificial, but the point of the exercise is to help you understand the difference between the descriptive and prescriptive approaches to language use.)

(Compare your comments with those supplied at the end of the book.)

LANGUAGE CHANGE, AND THE PROBLEM OF INTELLIGIBILITY

Language is dynamic: it changes as the world changes. If you look at the English used today, and compare it with English used a hundred years ago, there will be obvious differences. This is perfectly natural and understandable. For one thing, language needs to reflect the new ideas and things that have come into existence. Inventions such as the computer have brought a whole new set of vocabulary items into the English language. This is just one area of language change. Language change takes place for many diverse reasons and occurs in many different ways.

If language change is so natural and justifiable, why are so many people concerned and worried about the changes they detect in the languages they use? Did you find that your answers to the questions that we raised earlier in this chapter included reference to concerns, even fears, about language change?

Two of the main concerns that underlie resistance to language change are:

1 the tendency to see change as *deterioration* and decay, in other words, a concern about 'declining standards', and

2 the concern about lack of *mutual intelligibility* among language varieties, which refers to the tendency of language varieties to differ so much that the people using them cannot understand one another. (Would people from Britain, for example, understand the poem 'Da same, da same' as easily as a South African person who has some knowledge of the so-called Cape Coloured dialect?)

These concerns may sound familiar to you, as they are the kinds of issues often raised in the South African media, and in conversations and at meetings where teachers or parents of school-going children are present.

Unlike those who hold a pessimistic view of language change, people who are informed about language matters regard change as inevitable. It is neither good nor bad in itself, unless it leads to social divisions or lack of intelligibility. In such cases, language *planning* should be undertaken. More will be said about language planning in Chapter 4.

Effective communication should always be the guiding principle, and that is why schools should teach a 'common standard', while recognizing the value of other varieties. In this sense, 'standard' suggests *uniformity* for the purpose of understanding, and not a value judgement suggesting superior quality. As Trask puts it:

> ...[A]bove all, standard English is a *convenience*. Speakers from Glasgow, Newcastle, New Orleans and Cape Town are likely to have considerable trouble in understanding one another if they all insist in using their own local varieties of English. The existence of an agreed standard form, learned by all educated English-speakers everywhere, makes it much easier for all these people to talk to one another.[8]

However, we should also be aware that a 'totally uniform, regionally neutral ... variety of standard English does not yet exist worldwide'.[9] Even when people from different parts of the world communicate using the standard form of English, there will still be traces of linguistic features linked to the regions and national identities of the countries from which they come. The lexical and grammatical features would not, however, be so strong as to create mutual unintelligibility. But as we have seen, the phonological features, accent and pronunciation, are difficult to standardize and may still cause misunderstandings.

Activity 5 Non-standard English in the classroom

Imagine that you are a teacher, and that the speaker in the poem 'Da same, da same' had a child of school-going age who was in your class. How would you deal with the way this child would be likely to speak English? Substantiate your comments.

(Compare your ideas with the ones provided at the end of this book.)

SUMMARY

We would like to summarize the main points of this chapter as follows:
- There are different varieties of English in the world and in South Africa. The standard form enjoys the greatest prestige.
- We all have opinions and beliefs about language.
- The prescriptive view of language is concerned with, a perceived 'correctness'. It does not approve of non-standard varieties.

- The descriptive view of language is concerned with describing actual language usage.
- Language change cannot be avoided, and is not necessarily harmful to the development of language and its users.
- One form of a language (even the standard form) is no 'better' than any other form of that language, in linguistic terms. However, the individual who masters standard English is at a decided advantage.
- Using and teaching a standard form of a language is a practical way of helping all the people who use the language to understand one another, and to achieve 'mutual intelligibility'.
- Accent and pronunciation are difficult to change. Mutual intelligibility may be compromised by the accents of English additional-language speakers, even if these speakers are proficient in the other aspects of the language, such as English lexis and grammar.

GLOSSARY

Below you will find a list of some of the main terms referring to language concepts introduced in this chapter, together with brief explanations. We have also included some entries *without* explanations, for you to fill in for yourself. Try to show your own understanding of the terms, rather than simply copying definitions given in the chapter.

variety	one of the *forms* a language takes. The form depends on the circumstances in which the language is being used
standard variety	a fairly formal variety of English, usually the written form. This variety is used as a means of communication to link many peoples and countries of the world, and enjoys greater prestige than other, non-standard varieties
non-standard varieties	all varieties of English other than the standard, such as local vernacular forms; dialects that have lexical, grammatical and phonological deviations from standard English; and informal varieties that might include colloquialisms and slang

status (of a language) the standing or position of one language variety in relation to others; the degree of respect with which each variety is viewed

mutual intelligibility the ability of speakers (using two different varieties of a single language) to understand one another

accent _____

_____

dialect _____

_____

lexis _____

_____

syntax _____

_____

phonology _____

_____

prescriptive approach _____

_____

descriptive approach _____

_____

ENDNOTES

1 POTTER, A. 1987. *The context of literature written in English*, p. 12. Cape Town: Maskew Miller Longman.

2 POTTER, A. 1987. The context of literature written in English, p. 11 (adaption). Cape Town: Maskew Miller Longman.

3 SILVA, PENNY. 1997. 'The lexis of South African English: reflections of a multilingual society' in *Englishes around the world Vol 2*, p. 160, ed. Schneider, Edgar W. Amsterdam: John Benjamins.

4 CRYSTAL, DAVID. 1988. *The English language*, p. 24. Harmondsworth: Penguin Books.

5 'English - the language of a new nation: The present-day linguistic situation of South Africa' (1998) in

Even more Englishes: studies 1996-1997, p. 110. (Survey written by various contributors.) Amsterdam: John Benjamins.

6 QUIRK, RANDOLPH. 1993. 'Cultivate your lexicon if you know what I mean', 12 July. London: *The Times*.

7 CRYSTAL, DAVID. 1987. *The Cambridge Encyclopedia of Language*, p. 3. Cambridge: Cambridge University Press.

8 TRASK, R.L. 1995. *Language: the basics*, p. 174. London: Routledge.

9 CRYSTAL, DAVID. 1994. 'Which English, or English *which*?' in Mike Hayhoe and Stephen Parker, *Who owns English?* p. 113. Buckingham: Open University Press.

3   What do we use language for? Does it enable us to think?

CHAPTER OUTLINE

In this chapter, we examine the question 'What do we use language for?' and provide some answers to this question. This leads to a discussion of one of the functions of language that we identify: the importance of language in the process of thinking. We will discuss the *functions* of language generally, without referring to specific languages. However, we relate this discussion to South African society and South African language issues.

LEARNING OUTCOMES

By the end of this chapter you should be able to demonstrate the following knowledge, skills, values, and attitudes:

Knowledge

You should understand
- the various functions of language
- the relationship between language and thought
- the Sapir-Whorf hypothesis, and
- the relationship between language and categorization.

Skills

You should be able
- to demonstrate text-mapping skills by drawing a mind-map, and
- to reflect on your own thinking processes, and understand the extent to which these depend on language.

PART ONE
THE FUNCTIONS OF LANGUAGE[1]

1 Communication

Look at the following situations:
- A mine manager calls a meeting and informs his staff that the mine is closing down and jobs will be lost.
- A group of teenagers discuss their favourite music groups. *informal*
- A journalist writes a newspaper report about disastrous floods that have occurred in parts of KwaZulu-Natal. *Formal*
- Family members who have not seen one another for a long time exchange news at a family wedding.
- A friend tells you about a film she has enjoyed, based on a book she has read.
- A small child lets her mother know, in baby language, that she is hungry.

Such common examples of language use demonstrate that the most obvious purpose of language is to enable *communication*. The communicative function of language is the major purpose of language, but not the only one.

2 Emotional expression

Imagine that you are at home, writing out the final copy of an assignment you have been working on for some days. It is late at night but you are determined to finish it. The assignment has to be posted tomorrow. You reach for your ruler, and as you bring it towards your page, you knock over your mug of coffee. It runs all over the assignment pages, soaking them in a sticky brown liquid. You swear loudly, then repeat the swear words, <u>exclaiming</u> at your own stupidity.

What is the function of the language used in this instance? You are not communicating with another person, because you are alone in the room. You are communicating intrapersonally (with yourself), but you are also using another function of language: the *expression of emotion*.

Using emotive language is a means of 'letting off steam', or expressing how we feel when we are under stress. In the example just given, the emotions expressed are negative: anger and frustration. However, you could just as well exclaim with delight or admiration if you saw something beautiful, or saw someone doing something with great skill.

Let us return to the wider world of our multilingual society.

In what situations is language used most freely for the expression of emotions, and which languages are used? You probably thought of social situations involving home, family, friends, colleagues or even strangers. What language do you use to describe an emotional work situation when you get home in the evening? If you have children, what language do you use in your interaction with them, especially in situations involving emotion?

3 Social interaction

Imagine that you are walking along the pavement and see someone a few metres away whom you recognize, but do not know well. You lift your hand in greeting, call out 'Hi! How are you doing?' and carry on walking. Here again, language cannot be said to be performing the function of communicating ideas, because you are not really saying anything meaningful, nor do you necessarily expect a meaningful answer to your question.

The point here is that language is often used, not for any communicative purpose, but to maintain relationships between people. Different cultures have different 'rules' for what is considered acceptable language behaviour in specific social situations. Different social situations will call for different kinds of verbal behaviour. When you are with friends you have known for a long time, you will probably be very comfortable and relaxed and will use informal language, but in other perhaps more prestigious social gatherings you may be much more formal, and you will find that you are much more conscious of the way you speak.

Consider some of our stock social behaviour. Is there any meaning, for example, in the common English question 'How are you?'. Do people expect the stock reply 'Fine, thanks!', or do they really expect a detailed description of the other person's state of health? The kind of language use that functions only, or mainly, to 'oil the wheels of social interaction' is also known as *phatic communication*.

4 The power of sound

Sometimes people use words (either spoken or sung) just for the pleasure of hearing or making the sounds, or for other _effects_. This use of 'language' or human sound can only occur in its oral form (through speech, singing, or chanting). Thus, the power of the human voice is engaged in various ways. This use of language could encompass any of the entire range of sounds that the human voice is capable of making. Examples from different contexts are:

- *Religious ceremonies*: chanting and singing.
- *Politics*: persuasive speech-making by individuals; the shouting of chants or slogans by crowds at public demonstrations or on protest marches.
- *Physical work*: chanting by workers, presumably to establish a rhythm for the labour, and to build team morale.
- *Sports matches*: chanting songs or slogans at sports gatherings, such as soccer matches.
- *Marching*: whistling or singing marching songs by soldiers to keep time when they march, and to keep up morale.
- *Games*: playing with the sounds of language just for the enjoyment of it, such as the noises made by children when skipping or taking part in other playground games.
- *Singing*: producing sounds (of varying pitches, rhythms, tempos and volumes) for pleasure.

All members of society in South Africa are probably familiar with most, if not all of the above examples.

5 The control of reality

Consider the following examples of spoken language:
- 'I pronounce you husband and wife'
- 'I baptise you ...'
- 'I name this ship *The Gloriana*'
- 'I swear to tell the truth, ...'
- 'I declare the Games open ...'

These are a few examples of the *performative* function of language. When language is used in this way, it is not only used to communicate, but to *perform* an *action*. Somehow, pronouncing a certain verbal formula (saying a particular sequence of words) makes an occasion 'real' or properly ceremonial, or invests a certain event with truth or validity.

In some instances, a belief in the magical or sacred power of language plays a big role in some religious contexts. In other cases, using language in this way has the effect of bringing about a new psychological or social reality. In other words, language is used to *do* or to *change* something.

However, when someone uses language to do or change something, what is said may not always be called 'true' or 'untrue', since the words spoken may not always be a statement of fact. Think of the example 'The Republic of X ... declares war on ... '. This declaration represents an *action*, and calls for a *reaction*, rather than an agreement or disagreement.

Why is it sometimes important to *extract* a promise from someone, and to actually *hear* them speak the words 'I promise ... '? Why, in many countries, does a witness in court have to *verbally* take an oath before giving evidence? Do these situations reflect our deeply-rooted belief that words somehow have the power to *bind* the speaker to their promise or oath?

6   Recording the facts

A difficult issue arises in a workplace, where an employee believes her rights have been infringed upon. When investigating the case, the employer consults lawyers who study the laws embodied in the Constitution. The Constitution contains highly organized, clear, and explicit information, which has been written down to serve as a guide for all citizens. What use of language is the Constitution? Here, its function is to *record the facts*, and to state guidelines.

This is a very important use of language in society. It is obviously closely linked to the development of writing. (Such facts can also be recorded orally in the collective memory of a group, but less reliably.) The recording of history is one of the earliest examples of the use of language to perform this function.

Once again, it would be interesting to note which languages are used most often in South African society for this function. Think of the official records of Parliamentary proceedings, court records, government pronouncements, and electronic systems of knowledge storage and retrieval. All eleven official languages should be represented for the Constitution's recommendations to hold true.

7 The transfer of information (the transactional function)

Look at the following situations involving the transactional function of language:

- A teacher is standing in front of a class describing a new concept to the learners.
- You listen to the sports results on the radio to find out who won the soccer match.
- A woman refers to a recipe book as she makes supper in the kitchen.
- A government minister appears on television explaining a change in policy regarding the treatment of HIV/Aids.
- A child consults an encyclopedia to gather information for a school project.
- You would like to buy a second-hand car, and look up the relevant information in the classified section of the local newspaper.
- A pedestrian directs you to a place you are trying to find in town.

Language is the means by which we transfer information. Language enables us to carry out practical tasks. As students we use language to study. Such a language function makes learning possible. The kind of language used for this purpose is termed *referential language*. Referential language is used in all forms of teaching and instructing. The transfer of knowledge, skills and information is known as the *transactional* function of language.

8 The instrument of thought

Which comes first: *thought*, or the *words used to express thought*? This is a question that has puzzled philosophers, psychologists, and linguists for a long time. Commenting on the apparent dependence of thought on language, one humourist remarked: 'How can I know what I think unless I hear/see what I say?'

Later in this chapter, we will elaborate on the ways in which people use language to work through mental processes; to focus their concentration; or to clarify their thoughts.

9 The expression of identity

Think of a crowd of children gathered at an inter-school sports meeting. Each school has its own 'war cry', which the children shout together. Language here is being used to foster a sense of identity and to bind the group together. Chanting in this way builds up the spirit of the group and promotes a sense of pride in the school and in the sports game.

We tend to use specific languages, or specific varieties of the same language, in the relationships we have with different members of our family and various friends. Typically, young people have a particular vocabulary consisting of slang and colloquial phrases which mark them as members of a certain age group. At work you may express a certain identity associated with the use of a certain language.

There is a direct connection between one's *identity* and the *language* one uses. One's identity may be associated with different individuals and groups at different times, and in different contexts, for example, one may be a member of a religious group, a political group, or a group of supporters of a particular sporting team. Naturally, one may be a member of all these at once, and switch from one language or language variety to another within seconds.

Before we move on to the next topic, we would like you first to spend some more time thinking about the question of language and *identity*. You could ask yourself the following questions:

- What groups do people seem to be identifying with on particular occasions?
- What languages do they use to express their identity with each group?
- Do they use a particular language or language variety to exclude other people?
- What linguistic changes do individuals make as they change from one situation, relationship, or group, and move to another?

These questions are particularly interesting in a multilingual society, where languages and language varieties are likely to differ considerably from situation to situation.

We shall return to consider the connection between language and identity more fully in Chapter 5.

So far in this chapter, we have discussed the *functions* of language in the context of South African society, which is multilingual and thus offers people many opportunities to do different things with the various languages they know.

Activity 1 Text-mapping

Using the information you have learned in this chapter so far, draw a mind-map which clearly sets out the different *functions of language*.

(Compare your mind-map with the suggestions we make at the end of the book about how to go about drawing a mind-map.)

PART TWO
LANGUAGE AND THOUGHT

One of the functions of language we mentioned above is that it makes thought possible. There is a definite relationship between language and thought, although different people have their own ideas and opinions about this relationship. You might like to consider what opinions *you* have on this subject. The questions below may get you started.

- When you watch a baby responding to speech, do you think the baby has 'thoughts' which it is trying to 'put into words', or is it just trying to imitate sound?
- Have you ever wondered why people talk to themselves?
- In your opinion, which came first, human thought or human speech?
- If people all over the world have similar concepts and similar ideas, why do they speak different languages?
- How do deaf children learn to think if they cannot hear language?

These questions are really only a way of getting you to think about the relationship between language and thought. We do not answer these questions, but try to show how complex the relationship is between language and thought in the pages that follow. We would like you to consider whether language and thought are inseparably bound up with one another, or whether you think it is possible for the one to operate without the other. If language and thought are separate, which of the two is influenced by the other?

Activity 2 The relationship between language and thought: your own experience

To what extent, do you think, does language enable you to think rationally? Reflect on your behaviour when you have to solve a problem or perform some other rational act. Write about half a page in which you consider whether language is important to thought, giving specific examples from your own experience.

(Compare your thoughts on this personal topic with those given at the end of the book.)

Kinds of thinking

First, there are two kinds of thinking: thinking that does not involve language, and thinking that does. We could represent this distinction by means of a simple diagram:

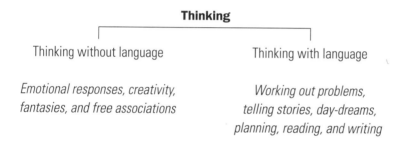

Thinking

Thinking without language

*Emotional responses, creativity,
fantasies, and free associations*

Thinking with language

*Working out problems,
telling stories, day-dreams,
planning, reading, and writing*

Here is an example to illustrate the difference between thought that involves language, and thought that does not. *Picture* or *imagine* yourself going home from work. Here you will be thinking *without* words. However, if you imagine yourself *directing* someone to your house from work, you will be thinking *with* words.

There are two kinds of thinking that involve language: *deductive* thinking (solving problems logically using a set of rules or a general law), and *inductive* thinking (solving problems logically and inferring a general law on the basis of particular information provided). We can refine our diagram to represent this more clearly:

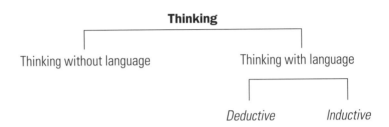

Let us now concentrate on the kind of thinking that *does* involve language.

Are language and thought independent of each other, dependent on each other, or identical with each other?

We are discussing *ideas* and *theories* about language, and need to bear in mind that not all theories can be proved absolutely 'right' or 'wrong'.

We are now considering the kind of thought that uses language. Let us think of the various theories as if they were positioned along a line stretching from one extreme to another:

On one end of the imaginary line lies one extreme theory that language and thought are totally separate, with one being dependent on the other. This theory is an 'hypothesis', or an idea that is not based on certainty. See the diagram below:

language and thought
are totally separate

language   thought

At the other end of the imaginary line lies the opposite view that language and thought are identical.

language and
thought are identical

If both positions are represented together on a diagram, it looks like this:

language and thought _____ language and
are separate thought are identical

┌──────────────┐
language　　　　　thought

The 'truth' (or reality) lies somewhere between these two extremes. On our diagram, this would be represented as follows:

language and thought _____ 'truth' _____ language and
are separate thought are identical

┌──────────────┐
language　　　　　thought

We now need to look at these beliefs, and their implications, in more depth:

Position 1
Language and thought are totally separate, and thought comes first

If you consider the possibility that language and thought are separate, it follows that one must be dependent on or linked to the other. There is a popular and widespread belief that thought comes first, and is then 'expressed' in words.

Position 2
Language and thought are totally separate, and language comes first

If you take this view, you believe that the ways in which people use language determine the ways in which they can think. For example, people who hold this view argue that children *first* learn a language, and *then* form concepts *using* that language. However, the fact that translations between languages are possible would seem to indicate that this is a rather extreme view.

Position 3
Language and thought are interdependent but not identical

This view holds that language and thought are not identical, but neither are they entirely separate either. Thought without words is possible (as described earlier in the chapter), but language remains a regular part of the process of thinking.

Position 4
Language and thought are identical

This is an extreme view, and is no longer common. We often think without words, so thought and language *can* be separated.

THE SAPIR-WHORF HYPOTHESIS

Let us now look in more detail at an example of Position 2 above. This position states that *language is believed to make thought possible*. This view has come to be known as the Sapir-Whorf hypothesis, also known as the 'theory of linguistic determinism'.

The Sapir-Whorf hypothesis takes its name from two scholars: the linguist and anthropologist Edward Sapir (1884–1939), and his pupil, Benjamin Lee Whorf (1897–1949). Their view states not only that our perception of the world influences our language, but also that the language we use profoundly affects how we think.

In terms of the Sapir-Whorf hypothesis, it was believed that language 'came first'. The languages developed by different societies are structured in particular ways. For example, many languages have *categories* of words such as nouns and verbs. These categories are used by all the members of those particular societies when they communicate, and form an essential part of the *patterns* and *systems* of those languages.

When members of human societies observe the world and natural phenomena around them, they make sense of what they see, and organize and explain it, by using the categories, patterns, and systems that exist in each language. In other words, they use language to *create concepts*.

As an illustration of this idea, you could think of the waves of the sea. In English and many other languages, this natural phenomenon is expressed in language by means of a noun. This is like saying that a wave is an object or thing, with the plural form *waves*.

However, in reality it is not physically possible to separate a single wave from the ones that go before or after it. Nor is it possible to observe a wave in a *static* form, as the sea is in constant motion. The idea that a wave is a 'thing' or object is just an *idea*, it exists only in the human mind, and is conveyed in some languages by means of the linguistic category called 'noun'. In other words, it is the *human mind*, using language, that 'divides nature up' into 'manageable parts' and organizes it, thereby gaining some measure of control in being able to describe each part. The wave example demonstrates this quite well, because there are some languages that do *not* use a noun to express the ceaseless motion of the sea.

The most extreme form of the Sapir-Whorf theory is no longer widely held. Some of the reasons against it may be summarized as follows:

- it is possible to translate ideas successfully from one language into another
- the concept and thought patterns of one language, even if they are unique, can be explained by using another language, and
- even in cases where a language lacks a word for a particular concept, its speakers can still understand that concept through the use of alternative words.

It is therefore no longer widely believed that language *determines* or controls the way we think. However, there does seem to be some evidence to support a 'weaker' version of the Sapir-Whorf theory: there is evidence to support a theory that suggests that language *influences* the way we think, rather than determining it. Examples of this influence include the following:

- language influences the way we perceive and remember: we use language to help us to understand and remember experiences
- language affects the ease with which we perform mental tasks: we use language to process information and to work out the steps in solving a problem, and
- if we can 'attach' a word or a phrase to something we need to remember, it is easier to recall it.

THE CONNECTION BETWEEN LANGUAGE AND ACADEMIC STUDY

Having seen how language facilitates mental functioning, comprehension, and the manipulation of ideas, it is clear that it must play a huge role in academic communication and study. The older, established languages, of which English is one, have the specialized vocabulary and terminology necessary for academic discourse. This is well and good, but what about our indigenous languages?

There are some reasons why many people feel that it is not possible to study in the African languages. For example, scientific and other specialized terminology does not yet exist in these languages. This issue relates to *language planning*, which will be fully discussed in the next chapter. It *is* possible for indigenous languages (as it has been for other languages) to develop to meet new academic thinking and other demands. This has already happened in the case of Afrikaans in South Africa, and is already happening in the African languages under the auspices of PANSALB (Pan South African Language Board). It is useful to remember that English too is a language that 'developed' from other languages, and continues to develop in order to meet the demands of, for example, technological development.

Following on our discussion about the relationship between language and thought, we shall consider how language makes it possible for us to categorize.

CATEGORIZATION

Consider the following sentences, and the highlighted words in them particularly.

*I need to buy some **furniture** for my flat.*
*We saw a lot of **game** when we went to the Kruger Park.*
*Several different **religions** are practised in this community.*
*The rand is weak in relation to many other overseas **currencies**.*

A little reflection makes us realize that each of the highlighted words is an 'umbrella term' for a number of separate things: a group of objects, creatures, or abstract concepts. These expressions demonstrate how normal it is for us to classify the things in our environment. Why do we do this?

Categorizing or classifying the millions of things that surround us is one method we human beings use to make sense of the diversity in the world around us. Grouping things into classes or categories is a form of simplification which helps us to understand and deal with all the people and objects in the world. This categorization activity satisfies a general human need. What, you may ask, has this to do with Language Studies?

Human categorization is both a *cognitive* process (a thought process) and a *linguistic* process (a process that uses language). A word like *furniture* is both a concept and a word. It names a group of items such as *sofa*, *chair* and *bed*. The human ability to conceptualize is largely dependent on language, because we have to use a linguistic term to *label* the concept. The lexical item or word that we use 'captures' the mental idea we have in mind. Categorization illustrates the close relationship between language and thought.

By its very nature, a category is an abstract notion. It may include concrete objects such as *sofa*, *chair*, and *bed*, but the concept of *furniture* is an abstract one. There is no single, concrete entity in the world that encapsulates the full meaning of the word *furniture*. This abstract category or class can only be referred to by means of a lexical item (a word). We are so familiar with this habit of categorizing ideas that we do not always realize that it is language that enables us to do so, but also that it is often a *particular* language, in this case, English. Not all languages categorize words relating to ideas in the same way. This fact possibly supports the Sapir-Whorf theory.

Hyponymy is the term that describes the kind of relationship between words that we have been discussing, for example, *sofa* is a hyponym of *furniture*. Words are *grouped* together, and then a name or 'heading' is given to the group. We can use the word 'inclusion' to describe the relationship between the heading and the words in the group. The members of the group are 'included' under the name of the group.

To illustrate, a *shirt* is a kind of clothing. *Jacket* and *trousers* are also kinds of clothing. *Clothing* is the category name, heading, or *superordinate* term (such as *furniture* in our earlier example). *Shirt, jacket,* and *trousers* are the *subordinate* terms that fall into the larger category.

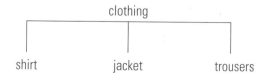

Another example: *anger* is a kind of emotion. *Emotion* is the category heading, and *anger* is a member of that category. Words like *fear* or *love* would also be members of the category, *emotion*. *Love* and *fear* would be on the same level as *anger*.

Now for a slightly more complex example. Read the following words: *psychology, mathematics, linguistics, physics, philosophy, chemistry,* and *history.*

Most people would have no trouble identifying these words as the names of specific disciplines or *fields of study*. In classifying the words this way, they would be using language as a way of *organizing ideas*. First of all, they would be *grouping* ideas. Simultaneously, they would be applying the idea of *levels*. The 'top' layer is the umbrella word or term: *fields of study*. This term is felt to be a larger concept of classification than the others in the above list. It is at a higher level than they are, and *includes* all of them. Look at the diagram below:

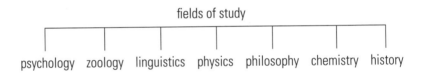

In this diagram, the *relationship* between the various ideas is indicated by means of language. We could use language to indicate a *further* or intermediary level of organization, as in the diagram below:

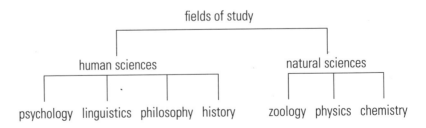

Here the words *human sciences* and *natural sciences* function as sub-headings, which group the items more precisely.

Activity 3 Categorization

Organize the words that follow into *categories*, using a *superordinate* term (a main heading) and *subheadings*, or intermediate terms:

Grapes, lamb, pumpkins, bread, squash, chicken, potatoes, oranges, beef, cereals, apples, and porridge.

(You will find our suggested answer to this activity at the end of the book.)

The ability or skill to organize and arrange aspects of our world is one that we need often, and perhaps most often in academic study. We use this skill when we summarize; when we express the main idea (or ideas) of a paragraph in key words; and when we write a paragraph with one topic sentence.

However, different languages categorize objects and ideas in different ways. It is important to realize that *the principles of classification that we apply come from the languages we use, and not from the real world.* It is a linguistic system, and not a real-world system of classification.

SUMMARY

Here is a summary of the main points discussed in this chapter:
- Language performs many different functions in human life.
- These functions include communication, emotional expression, social interaction, the enjoyment of sound, the control of reality, the recording of facts, the transfer of information, the expression of identity, and the ability to think.
- Language is central to the complex process of thinking.
- The Sapir-Whorf theory holds that thought is entirely dependent on language.
- Opinions vary as to the extent to which language facilitates thought processes.

- It is possible to develop newly literate languages so that they may be used in academic discourse. This involves language planning.
- Language enables us to conceptualize and categorize information.

GLOSSARY

The list below contains most of the important terms dealt with in this chapter. Fill in your own explanations in the spaces provided. Try to show your own understanding of the terms, rather than simply copying definitions given in the chapter.

language functions _____
_____

referential use of language _____
_____

transactional function of language _____
_____

phatic communication _____
_____

performative use of language _____
_____

hypothesis _____
_____

Sapir-Whorf hypothesis _____
_____

hyponymy _____
_____

superordinate _____
_____

subordinate _____
_____

ENDNOTES

1   This discussion on 'The functions of language' is adapted from David Crystal's discussion in *The Cambridge Encyclopedia of Language*, Chapter 4. 1987. Cambridge: Cambridge University Press.

4 Which English variety for official use?

CHAPTER OUTLINE

In Chapters 1 and 2 we discussed how the dominance of one language (English) in South Africa is often regarded as unjust, since all eleven official languages have equal status according to the Constitution.

The situation in which languages do not seem to be treated or regarded as equal can be addressed by means of *language planning*. In this chapter, we will discuss language planning and its place in government policy.

LEARNING OUTCOMES

By the end of this chapter you should be able to demonstrate the following knowledge, skills, values, and attitudes:

Knowledge

You should understand
- the nature of a multilingual society
- the role and function of official languages within society
- the function of language planning, and
- the two types of language planning.

Skills

You should be able
- to summarize and compare different viewpoints
- to distinguish between the principles underlying different arguments, and
- to express your own opinion.

Values and attitudes

You should develop
- objectivity in describing different viewpoints, and maintain respect and tolerance for linguistic diversity.

INTRODUCTION

The question 'Why do we use language?' can be looked at as part of a more complex question: '*Who* uses *which language(s),* and for *what purpose(s)?*' The more complex question has three components with a relationship between them:

1 **Identity** ('who?')
2 **Language choice** ('which language?')
3 **Function** ('for what purpose?')

We would like to look at the question of *identity* in the context of South African society. Read the following quotation from the book *Language and social history*[1], edited by Rajend Mesthrie.

> My father's home language was Swazi, and my mother's home language was Tswana. But as I grew up in a Zulu-speaking area we used mainly Zulu and Swazi at home. But from my mother's side I also learnt Tswana well. In my high school I came into contact with lots of Sotho and Tswana students, so I can speak these two languages well. And of course I know English and Afrikaans. With my friends I also use Tsotsitaal.

The person whose words are quoted above is a 23-year-old male student from Germiston in Gauteng. During the official South African census of 1991, he was asked to indicate the languages in which he was proficient. The editor of the book points out that the speaker is not unusual in his ability to use many languages. In fact, many people in South Africa use several languages.

A society such as South African society is called a *multilingual* society. This means that many languages are spoken by the people who live within its borders. The language they choose to use on a particular occasion depends on the context, and the purpose for which they are using the language.

As we have seen, the fact that South Africa has eleven official languages is problematic. However, the linguistic difficulties encountered in our multilingual society are not new. These difficulties did not begin with the changes of 1994. Many thinking people have grappled for a long time with the issue of how best to manage the multilingual composition of our society, and have reacted in different ways.

There is an interesting example from South African history that may have affected the number of indigenous languages now in existence. Before local African languages were written down for the first time, certain groups of people spoke languages that were closely related to one another, with only minor differences. These similarities could be found in grammar and lexis (vocabulary).

Some linguists feel that when these languages were given a written form, these differences were exaggerated. In other words, the differences were made to seem more important than they really were at the time. After being written down, these languages developed standard forms. The result is that in certain cases we now have separate languages where there might have been only one language with regional dialects. Some linguists feel that this has created unnecessary fragmentation and divisions between peoples who are related and should be closer to one another. Many linguists have also suggested that these languages should aim to move closer to one another once again, and become a single standard language with regional variants.

This issue is discussed in the extract[2] below:

In 1944, the headmaster of Wilberforce Institute, Jacob Nhlapo, who was also a member of the ANC, wrote an article entitled 'Bantu Babel: Will the Bantu languages live?' in the series called *The Sixpenny Library* ... . Essentially, Nhlapo proposed that the spoken varieties of Nguni and Sotho respectively be standardised in a written form as the first step to a possible standardised indigenous African language, in order to help to overcome tribal and ethnic divisions. While this process was being initiated and nurtured by all possible means, English should be promoted as the *lingua franca*. In his own words:

Which do you think is going to be easier to do: to get all African children to go to the school where they will all learn English, or to build out of the many Bantu languages in South Africa at least two mother tongues, Nguni and Sotho, and to get all the Africans to love and freely use them?

English ought to be made the African 'Esperanto'* while the question of the African Babel of tongues is being cleared up. Even when we have been able to make Nguni and Sotho the two mother tongues, if ever we do manage to do this, English will still be the African 'Esperanto'. Even if we do not manage to build one joint Bantu language or two, English will still be the answer to the question of the many Bantu tongues as it has been in America, where nations from all parts of Europe and from Africa found themselves living together.

*'Esperanto' was an artificial language invented in 1887 as a means of international communication, based on the European languages but with easy grammar and pronunciation. In this article, Nhlapo uses 'Esperanto' to refer to the use of English in South Africa as a common language or *lingua franca*.

The reason we have quoted this early suggestion of Nhlapo's is that it represents an unofficial but acute awareness that some sort of language planning was necessary to facilitate communication in our linguistically diverse country.

It is worth noting that Nhlapo's proposal to reduce the several African languages to two main languages, and to promote English as the *lingua franca* in South Africa, is directly opposed to the thinking of Ngugi wa Thiong'o whom we quoted in Chapter 1. Ngugi feels that it is crucially important that all the African languages be preserved as primary languages, and that the use of English among Africans should be discouraged.

OFFICIAL USES OF LANGUAGE

Many countries around the world are multilingual. However, even though multilingualism is so widespread, many people in Western countries are unaware of this and *think* it is common to have only one language in a country. This is because *government policies* create that impression, by giving special status to only one language. This language is then conveniently known as the *official language* of the country, and is used for official or government purposes.

As we know, South Africa currently recognizes eleven official languages.

Where would you expect to find examples of the *official* use of a language or languages? We have started a list below. As you encounter more examples, make a note of them.

- Notices in government buildings (such as law courts, and labour offices)
- Government gazettes
- Official circulars from government departments (such as the national education ministry or department, and provincial education departments)
- Advertisements for staff for government departments (such as the revenue services, labour, and water affairs)
- National Grade 12 external examination papers

These examples are instances in which you would expect to find the official languages of a country being used (no matter what country you are talking about). In South Africa, would you find that all eleven official languages are used in these official documents on a day-to-day basis? No. It is English that is most often used, sometimes together with Afrikaans and a 'regional' African language (according to the province in which the document appears). There is usually a note on each government document inviting members of the public to request a copy in one of the other eleven official languages if they wish.

As we discussed in Chapter 3, one of the primary functions of language is to *communicate*. Now consider those areas of life in which the communicative function of language is most prevalent. Which languages are used in these areas?

Think about *newspapers*: they use language to convey information (although that is not their only function). Which languages are most commonly used in South African newspapers?

Does the picture change when you look at the use of the languages used on *radio*? How many languages are used on the various radio stations for presenting the news?

What about *education*? Which languages are used? What do you notice about language choice in the schools with which you are familiar? Are the 'content subjects' taught in English, or in the non-English primary language of the majority of learners?

What about the language or languages of the *workplace*? Which languages are used to convey instructions, and to give explanations of procedures?

Activity 1 The use of official languages in South Africa

Collect as many examples as you can of official uses of the various languages of South Africa, such as the examples above. Enter your examples in the table below:

Language name	Item or context, and name of government department (or other authority)	National or provincial?

Which language, and for what purpose?

Mesthrie[3] looks at the question of the use of language from a *functional* point of view. What are the functions that people need to perform with language? Which language do they choose for each function?

A present-day functional profile of the languages of South Africa would show a hierarchy, however, with English dominant in commerce, higher education, industry and now in government; and Afrikaans dominant, until recently, in the civil service and government, and in the police, army and navy. African languages have not, however, been silent in public life. They are used as media of instruction in primary schools catering for African pupils, sometimes unofficially even after the switch-over to English by the fifth year of schooling. For matriculation in these schools English and an African language are required subjects. Apartheid broadcasting created nine separate radio stations for African languages and a television channel for Zulu-Xhosa and Sotho-Tswana, which ought to prosper further in a democratic climate. The recent designation of eleven languages as official in South Africa ... is clearly going to challenge the old colonial and apartheid linguistic hierarchy.

Language questions are always troublesome to governments. People feel strongly about their languages, which are part of their identity as human beings. Each group of people in various countries wants to promote its particular language, and this often gives rise to violent protests about government language policies they do not agree with. An obvious example of such a clash took place in South Africa in 1976, when black schoolchildren rebelled against being made to study through the medium of Afrikaans.

A more recent case involved some policemen who insisted on using their primary tongues, Tswana and isiZulu, in the course of their duties, claiming that this was their right, since all (eleven official) languages were equal according to the Constitution. The case was brought to the Pretoria High Court, and judge Marius de Klerk ruled against the policemen, stating that the applicants' suggestion was not practical, and that if case books and dockets were completed in everybody's language, 'there could be no effective communication to make police services accessible to all'. The judge referred to the South African Constitution (Act 108 of 1996)[4] and made the important distinction between 'esteem' and 'use'. He stated that 'all languages enjoy parity of esteem, not parity in use. If the use of all mother languages were allowed, it would be chaos'. He concluded that 'the campaign of the applicants' to have Standing Order 201 of the South African Police Service (governing the restricted use of language in police dockets, reports, and occurrence books) declared unconstitutional 'was reprehensible and endangered law and order'. (*Pretoria News*, 9 March, 1998). This judgement was a significant one and has set a precedent regarding the issue of which official language(s) may be used in the government services.

In order to try to avoid such conflicts in law, governments often engage in deliberate *language planning*.

LANGUAGE PLANNING

What is language planning? It involves *creating and implementing an official policy* for languages. Government states which languages are going to be used and in what ways they should be used. The language planners make critically important decisions during the planning. These decisions are not simple to make, since planners have to take into account many historical, political, economic, religious, educational, and social factors. The debates surrounding each of these factors cannot be settled easily.

There are two types of language planning: *status planning*, where decisions are made regarding the way in which a language is to be used in society, and *corpus planning*, which entails the planning of linguistic structure or use. This distinction reflects two different language policy areas in which the South African authorities are currently involved.

• Status planning

This involves the decisions made by government regarding the *use* of various languages in all areas of public life. For example, countries that gained independence from colonial powers during the twentieth century had to decide which languages were to be used for their official purposes (in education and courts of law, for example). The designation of the eleven official languages in the Constitution of South Africa is an example of *status planning*.

• Corpus planning

This involves decisions taken by the authorities to develop or change the *structure* of the language itself. Corpus planning develops new vocabulary, for example. Some governments have official terminology committees who are responsible for officially extending the vocabulary of a language, to enable its speakers to express concepts in areas such as modern science and technology, as efficiently as possible.

PANSALB

The Pan South African Language Board (PANSALB) is the official body appointed to carry out language planning in South Africa. PANSALB is an independent statutory body set up by government to promote multi-lingualism. It is useful to know about the sort of work this body does, and the kinds of issues it deals with.

An address by Christa Roodt, a spokesperson for PANSALB, gives a good indication of the vision and the scope of their work:[5]

> PANSALB's goal is always that of maximising multilingual communicative competence, rather than increasing language barriers amongst people. This is particularly relevant for processes at local community level.
>
> Languages co-exist ... They cannot and should not be compartment-alised. Also, no single language, not even English as the linking language, can fulfil the varied and diverse needs of all local authorities and their constituencies at all times and for all purposes. Multilingualism does not imply the use of all eleven languages at all times in all situations. It most definitely does not imply [a] badly planned multiplication of language services. It does ask of us to expend energy ... to be the best citizens we can be; thus, taking the trouble to plan carefully and responsibly; taking the trouble of assessing constituencies, and modernising those languages presently prevented from functioning in domains such as regional and local economies. Functional multilingualism, at local government level, pre-supposes that citizens should receive essential information in languages that they understand. Local government will need to identify the appropriate medium of communication, otherwise citizens may continue to feel like strangers in their local communities.

An important aspect of PANSALB's brief is to develop the previously marginalized languages. This initiative relates to *corpus planning* (involving the development of terminology, lexicography and litera-ture). Dr Mike Tlale of PANSALB believes it is a 'myth' that African languages cannot be used as official languages of tuition at institutions of learning. Speaking at a ceremony at the University of Pretoria to honour students who had excelled in African language courses, he stated that 'if there were people who still believed that African languages could not be developed [for] ... use [in] science and economics, such people needed to be informed of studies being conducted worldwide into the development of languages'.[6]

Another one of PANSALB's functions is to investigate cases where people are dissatisfied with official language use. PANSALB invites all citizens of South Africa to submit complaints about language use. The following invitation can be found on their website (http://www.pansalb.org.za).

Know your language rights!

Have your language rights been violated? Have you ever been subjected to linguistic domination, division and discrimination? Do you know of any person whose language rights have been violated? Do you [know to whom] … those complaints can be directed …? The Pan South African Language Board created by the Constitution, and the Pan South African Language Board Act No. 59 of 1995 … [are] at your service at all times to ensure that your language rights are realised. To report any language rights violation complaint, or for further information about your language rights call Tel no: 012-341 9638/9651 or Fax: 012-341 5938.

This is an authentic complaint of the sort that PANSALB receives and investigates:

Mr. A. E. van Niekerk has submitted a complaint to the Board to the effect that the Premier and the Speaker of the Northern Cape have violated Section 6 of the Constitution Act, 1996 (Act No. 108 of 1996), which makes provision for eleven official languages, and mandates the state to take practical measures and positive steps to elevate the status and advance the use of these languages. Mr van Niekerk's language rights violation complaint against the Premier and the Speaker centred around the following: that the Premier of the Northern Cape discriminated against all official languages except English at its opening ceremony on 20 February 1998 by:

1   sending out only English invitations … [for] the official opening
    of the sixth session of the First Legislature of the Northern Cape
    Province

2   conducting his speech in English and including only short
    paragraphs in Afrikaans and Setswana, and

3   welcoming the guests at lunch primarily in English.

In spite of the efforts of PANSALB, English remains the favoured language, as we have seen. A study conducted by the 'Friday Group', an independent language group, looked at eight main areas of language usage, and found that the language injunctions of the Constitution are being disregarded in a manner which at times borders on 'defiance'. It released the following figures:

- Pamphlets and booklets printed between 1994 to 1999 showed there was an 88% decline in Sepedi pamphlets, a 70% decline in Afrikaans, a 60% decline in isiZulu, but a 34% increase in English.

- Programming on SABC's TV 1, 2 and 3 between April 2000 and June 2000 was 74% English, 8,9% Afrikaans, 8,4% multilingual, 4,79% Nguni languages and 3,4% Sotho.

Pretoria News, 12 November, 2001

So, statistics confirm that the other official South African languages take a back seat to English. Unquestionably, English is the official language most often used.

This brings us back to the question of variety, and which variety of English is used for official purposes. Although standard English would seem the obvious choice because of the need for mutual intelligibility, not everyone agrees that this variety is the most desirable. Some feel that a distinct form of English, that could be called South African English, already exists, and that this form should be actively promoted, as it expresses a uniquely South African experience and culture. You may recall that in Chapter 2, we quoted Crystal's statement that 'a totally uniform, regionally neutral variety does not yet exist worldwide'. This implies that it would be futile to try to eliminate from the different varieties of English around the world the features that make them nationally and even regionally distinctive. English cannot be 'wrenched' from its non-English geographical location.

HOW MUCH DEVIATION SHOULD BE TOLERATED?

It is all very well to talk vaguely about 'South African English', but if we are going to use a spoken variety of English with distinctively South African features, which variety will this be? We have already established that there is more than one distinctively South African variety of English. The other question that arises is: how much deviation will be acceptable? We do not want to compromise the centrally important principle of mutual intelligibility. What degree of deviation should be tolerated? Who is going to determine the limits?

Should we, for example, accept the following non-standard usages in radio or television broadcasting?

Eat finished *before you leave the table.*
I am *packing out* *my cupboard.*
When you're tired of playing with the toys, put *it* *away.*
She was *busy dying* *of pneumonia.*
After the tennis match, her *one leg* *was sore.*
My wife *she* *is a teacher.*
I walked into the shop and I saw *this* *assistant smoking.*
Don't worry; we'll *make a plan.*
He was a very poor *somebody* *at that time of his life.*
He's not allowed *doing* *that.*
She went *with* *the aeroplane.*
I asked him why *did he go.*
Others *were dancing,* *others* *were talking.*
I'm sleeping *by* *her house tonight.*
I *am having* *a problem.*
I need to buy *a pants.*
I can use *a scissor.*
It *can* *be that she's getting sick.*
I was *for a long time* *away.*
My husband is *late* *(meaning dead).*
There are *less* *people here tonight than last night.*
What time you saw him?
I don't know when *is he* *coming home.*
If you don't *come right* *with your problem, come back to me.*
Since *I'm* *in Pretoria, for five years I* *lived* *in this house.*
I haven't seen you for a long time. Why are you so *scarce?*
You should try *by all means* *to get a distinction in that subject.*
He was *a twin.*
He told me the news last week *already.*
There's *five children in the family.*
I'll see you *just now* *(meaning shortly, not a moment ago).*
Go this afternoon, *rather.*
Because, why?

The examples of the non-standard usage of 'somebody' and 'late' given above are common among English additional-language speakers and some English primary-language speakers in South Africa. We have said that all languages change over time and that change is not necessarily disadvantageous or wrong. Should such non-standard usages be simply accepted as part of the process of the natural evolution of language, normal, and inevitable? Or do you think we should reject them because they threaten to undermine 'correct' English usage? Questions like these continue to occupy linguists and academics.

Many of these expressions are widely used and accepted in South Africa but would sound very odd to British- or American English-speakers, for example. This proves that (a) distinctively South African variety (or varieties) of English does/do exist. While one is reluctant to label them 'errors' in a rigidly prescriptive way, and teachers of English would probably hold different opinions about their acceptability, it is worth noting that such usages would be edited out of a manuscript intended for publication both locally and overseas.

When talking of non-standard usage, we perhaps need to emphasize the distinction between *lexis* and *grammar* again. An example of the use of the word *gatvol*, which will be discussed shortly, is a matter of *lexis*, because it is a particular *item of vocabulary*. Some of the other examples we listed above, however, are more complicated, and concern *grammatical construction*. Among these are:

> *Eat finished before you leave the table.*
> *I am **packing out** my cupboard.*
> *When you're tired of playing with the toys, put **it** away.*
> *She was **busy dying** of pneumonia.*
> *After the tennis match, her **one leg** was sore.*
> *My wife **she** is a teacher.*

The standard English versions of the above examples have been supplied below, with brief explanatory comments.

> *Eat finished before you leave the table.*
> ***Finish eating** before you leave the table.*
> (The former is a direct translation from the Afrikaans *eet klaar*.)

*I am **packing out** my cupboard.*
*I am **unpacking** my cupboard.*
(The former is a direct translation from the Afrikaans *uitpak*.)

*When you're tired of playing with the toys, put **it** away.*
*When you're tired of playing with the toys, put **them** away.*
(There is a lack of concord in the former: confusion between singular and plural: lack of noun/pronoun agreement. This arises from the fact that *dit* in Afrikaans can be singular or plural.)

*She was **busy dying** of pneumonia.*
*She was **dying** of pneumonia.*
(The former is a direct translation from the Afrikaans word *besig* to denote the present continuous tense: *Sy was besig om dood to gaan*. In English, the word *busy* refers specifically to a person or people in a situation full of physical/mental activity or application, or to being energetically occupied, which is not applicable to a dying patient.)

*After the tennis match, her **one leg** was sore.*
*After the tennis match, her **leg** was sore.*
(If we use the phrase *one leg*, we imply that the person has only one leg. After all, *leg* is already singular, so it is confusing to read the redundant word *one*. We realize that the first sentence above is wrong, if taken literally, because a one-legged person cannot possibly play tennis.)

*My wife **she** is a teacher.*
My wife is a teacher.
(The former shows an African language influence. In African languages it is essential to add the pronoun after the noun.)

Now, think of the word *gatvol*, a distinctively South African word. The *Oxford South African Dictionary* defines *gatvol* as follows:

gatvol
adj. South African informal: extremely fed up or disgusted, ORIGIN from Afrikaans *gat* 'anus, arse' + *vol* 'full'

Would you regard *gatvol* as an acceptable South African English word, suitable for official purposes? Read the following:

Gatvol slips into Parliament's lexicon

AN MP CAN say *gatvol* in Parliament, but cannot call another MP a racist, a liar, a lesbian, or a bush-tick on an ox's tail.

The latter may be a colourful turn of phrase, but one which in 1940 drew a stern admonition from the Speaker's chair for the MP who uttered it to withdraw the remark.

This week, the word *gatvol* only just made it into the records, being ruled "not unparliamentary" by deputy chairman of committees, Dr Kisten Rajoo.

He was asked by ANC MP Zhou Kota to rule on whether New National Party MP Keppies Niemann should have been allowed to say that, just as an ANC speaker had said the government was *gatvol* of farmers, millions of law-abiding citizens were *gatvol* of people like murderers, rapists and taxi operators who trampled the rights of others.

Consulting a dictionary, Dr Rajoo said the expression translated as "fed up to the back teeth" and said parliamentary officials had advised him it was not on the official list of unparliamentary expressions, so he allowed it.

The question of unparliamentary language is symbolic of the extent to which Parliament is still in transition.

The official list which Parliament uses dates from before 1994, a different era when Parliament was sovereign and the Constitution was not, when there were two official languages and not 11, and when it was defamatory to call someone a communist, and racism was government policy ...

Pretoria News, 2 April, 2001

The acceptance of the word *gatvol* for official purposes is interesting for more than one reason. First, it is an example of *borrowing* from another language, in this case Afrikaans. The South African variety of English has been enlarged by borrowings from a number of different indigenous languages. *Gatvol* has now become one of these, an Afrikaans word used and understood by people speaking English in an English parliamentary debate.

Second, *gatvol* might be considered to be a rather vulgar colloquialism, yet it is being used and accepted by members of the government in the Houses of Parliament. This is an unexpected context for the use of this word, and reflects the fact that attitudes have relaxed in some ways. At one time *gatvol* would have been considered too informal and disrespectful. How do *you* feel about the use of *gatvol* in this particular context? Should we endorse the inclusion of words like *gatvol* for official purposes? Or do you think that once again we should reject them because they undermine 'correct' English usage?

In other respects, however, conventions applied to the way language is used in official contexts today are more strict than those applied fifty years ago. People are no longer free to fling racial terms at one another at random (as we will be discussing more fully in Chapter 7), or to make sexist remarks. As the final part of the article quoted above indicates, the prevailing political order directly influences perceptions about what is acceptable language use and what is not.

The extracts below are from various journal articles in which these issues of acceptability are discussed. Some of them are very brief, but they do, nevertheless, express various distinct opinions on the subject. The extracts are followed by activities. We hope that these activities will encourage you to think more about the issues we have been discussing in this chapter.

Where necessary, some of the terms which may be unfamiliar have been explained in notes below each excerpt.

1   The first quotation is from the first English Academy lecture, delivered by Es'kia Mphahlele[7] in 1984.

> ... [N]o one owns a language to the extent that they can limit or control or monitor the direction it will take on the lips of other users beyond its national boundaries. We appropriated these colonial languages, domesticated them in order to express an African sensibility, traditional, modern, rural or urban, political or religious ... .

- *appropriated*   took and used as our own
- *sensibility*   feeling

2 In the second English Academy lecture, delivered in 1985, Guy Butler[8] replied as follows:

> … English has become *de facto* the *lingua franca* of South African politics … the advantage must go to the international language … it is indispensable in a way that our other languages are not.
>
> … unlike the other SA languages, English will be everybody's … the opportunities for plain misunderstanding alone are frightening.
>
> … all those who have English as a birthright or have adopted English because they need it have a vital common interest in looking after it: to prevent the development of grammatical or phonetic variants so marked that it ceases to be a means of communication, not only with South Africa but with the rest of the world.

- *de facto*   in fact
- *variant*   one of a set of alternative forms

3 Njabulo Ndebele[9] replied to these remarks in the Keynote Address at the Jubilee Conference of the English Academy of Southern Africa in 1986:

> … [S]ome renowned thinkers, who are native speakers of English, have observed … that … the development of English in various parts of the world has taken forms that have gone beyond the control of the native speakers … [and] that English is no longer the exclusive property of its native speakers. …
>
> There are at least two possible responses of the native speakers of English to this seemingly inevitable process. They may celebrate, in the spirit of international linguistic democracy, the birth of new languages based on the English language; or, they may descend into fits of anxiety, firstly over the purported mutilation of their language with the possible attendant loss of intelligibility, and secondly, over the fear of the loss of influence.
>
> … I think that we cannot afford to be uncritically complacent about the role and future of English in South Africa, for there are many reasons why it cannot be considered an innocent language. The problems of society will

also be the problems of the predominant language of that society, since it is the carrier of a range of social perceptions, attitudes and goals.

… South African English must be open to the possibility of its becoming a new language. This may happen not only at the level of vocabulary…, but also with regard to grammatical adjustments … .

- *purported*   claimed
- *mutilation*   damage
- *complacent*   self-satisfied

4 More recently, Peter Titlestad addressed the issue of standard English in a journal article.[10]

… [W]hat departures from the international standard does one choose to codify as the new South African English? What are the characteristics of this new English? … Standard Ten school leavers … show in their usage a wide range of frequent basic errors … This South African English would be utterly disempowering for any serious purpose and might not even make a very reliable local *lingua franca*.

Professor Njabulo Ndebele, in his well-known Keynote address to the English Academy conference of 1986 (Ndebele: 1987) … said menacingly that English in South Africa would become a new language, not only lexically but grammatically. Did he really understand what he was saying, in his own impeccably-phrased standard English?

… [A]ttitudes to English must be positive and the prejudice against standard English must be exorcised. … Of course, various forms of South African English exist, but standard English must be the target language for schools.

- *codify*   put into a system of rules
- *lexically*   as regards vocabulary

5 The following excerpt is from an article by Tom McArthur,[11] in which he reviews 'the kinds of dictionaries now being created to cope with English as a universal language':

… [T]he globalisation of English in general and Standard English in particular began decades ago … And this supranational state of affairs will soon be altogether clear when the world's linguistic demography shows that more non-natives than natives use English with educated success….

[T]he phrase 'English as an international language' (EIL) ... fits in with a development which has recently become widely recognised and is now probably irreversible: that everyone who uses English (native or foreign) has to negotiate its standard forms at an international level.

- *globalisation*   becoming worldwide
- *supranational*   international
- *linguistic demography*   the spread and distribution of languages

---

Activity 2 Summary of extracts from articles

The five articles above express various opinions about standard English. In the table below, you will find a summary of each of these five extracts in the left-hand column. They are not in the same order as the given articles.

    The name of the author should appear in the right-hand column next to the summary of the extract from each article. The right-hand column has been left blank in each case for you to fill in the name of the relevant author.

Summary	Name of Author
1 Standard English is most appropriate for the South African situation and must be taught in South African schools. Any other form of English would not help South African learners to advance as far as they would like to.	
2 English in South Africa must change to suit the South African situation. Even the grammar must change.	
3 Because English is a world language, all those who use it for international purposes must use standard English.	
4 English has already changed to suit the African situation, and it will continue to change in ways that cannot be controlled.	
5 People who use English in South Africa must use its standard forms. They must protect the language and take care not to allow it to change.	

(Compare your answer with our answers at the end of the book.)

Activity 3 Language change

The five extracts quoted above all express an opinion about language change. Some of the authors feel that change *cannot* be avoided, others feel that it *must* be avoided.

Read the extracts again and then arrange them in the *correct* order, according to the authors' feelings about change. We have drawn a line below, with spaces along it in which you can write the names of the relevant authors. We have also provided a key with a brief description of each opinion, to help you in your thinking.

The name of the author who *strongly* believes that English *should* change for the South African situation should appear in the space on the extreme left. The name of the author who, in your opinion, is most strongly *opposed* to change should appear in the space on the extreme right.

Now try this activity, and then compare your opinions with those given at the end of this book.

feels very strongly
that English *should*
change

feels very strongly
that English *should not*
change

| Author 1 | Author 2 | Author 3 | Author 4 | Author 5 |
| .... | .... | .... | .... | .... |

Author 1 feels very strongly that English *should* change.
Author 2 *accepts* that English will change.
Author 3 feels that standard English should be used.
Author 4 feels that English should be *protected* from change.
Author 5 feels strongly that English *should not* change.

(Compare your answer with our suggested answer at the end of the book.)

Activity 4 Your own opinion

1 What are your thoughts about the question of official language choice?
2 How do you think the official policy of multilingualism should be implemented in South Africa?
3 What do *you* think would be the best for South Africa and South Africans, especially learners? Write a paragraph in which you give your opinion on this matter.

SUMMARY

Here is a summary of the main points discussed in this chapter:

- South Africa is a multilingual country with eleven official languages.
- Decisions about which language to use, and for what purpose, are complex, and are influenced by many factors.
- Conflicts and disputes sometimes arise because people do not agree with the way official languages are used.
- Language planning has to be carried out in order to control what happens to languages in a country, and to officially sanction certain changes.
- Language planning involves status planning and corpus planning.
- Opinions differ about which variety of English should be used for what official purposes in South Africa. Some believe that only standard English should be used, while others feel that a variety with distinctively South African features should be accepted.

GLOSSARY

Write down your own explanations next to the most important terms used in this chapter. You may wish to add other terms of your own.

multilingual   _____

_____

language planning   _____

_____

corpus planning   _____
                        _____

status planning   _____
                        _____

Esperanto   _____
                        _____

PANSALB   _____
                        _____

ENDNOTES

1 MESTHRIE, RAJEND (ed). 1995. *Language and social history. Studies in South African sociolinguistics.* Cape Town: David Philip.

2 ALEXANDER, N. 1989. *Language Policy and national unity in South Africa/Azania*, pp. 12, 22 and 32. Cape Town: Buchu Books.

3 MESTHRIE, RAJEND (ed). 1995. *Language and social history. Studies in South African sociolinguistics*, p. xvii. Cape Town: David Philip.

4 South Africa. 1996. The Constitution of the Republic of South Africa, Act 108, Section 6, No. 4. Cape Town and Pretoria: Government Printer.

5 PANSALB.Conference on 'Multilingualism in South African cities and towns: ideals and realities', 7–9 October 1999.

6 *Pretoria News*, 2 April, 2001.

7 MPHAHLELE, ES'KIA. 1984. 'Prometheus in chains: the fate of English in South Africa' in *The English Academy Review 2*, November, p. 90.

8 BUTLER, GUY. 1986. 'English in the new South Africa' in *The English Academy Review 3*, (month unspecified) pp. 173–74.

9 NDEBELE, NJABULO. 1987. 'English and social change' in *The English Academy Review 4*, January, pp. 12–13.

10 TITLESTAD, PETER. 1998. 'South Africa's language ghosts' in *English Today 54*, Vol. 14, No. 2, April, pp. 33–39.

11 MCARTHUR, TOM. 1998. 'Guides to tomorrow's English', in *English Today*, 55, Vol. 14, No. 3, July, pp. 21–26.

5 How does language reveal who we are?

CHAPTER OUTLINE

In this chapter we consider the ways in which language is linked to our personal and group identity. We are going to consider *idiolects* and *dialects*.

LEARNING OUTCOMES

By the end of this chapter you should have the following knowledge, skills, values, and attitudes:

Knowledge

You should understand
- the relationship between language and identity
- the meaning of the term *idiolect*
- the meaning of the term *dialect*
- that individual English speech features are shaped by factors such as region, primary language (if other than English), age, gender, social position, and
- that different South African dialects show the influence of different indigenous languages.

Skills

You should be able
- to describe the characteristic features of a particular idiolect, and
- to recognize a dialect and describe its linguistic characteristics.

Values and attitudes

You should develop
- sensitivity to, and respect for, individual differences in language use (in idiolect and dialect).

INTRODUCTION

Often without realizing it, we reveal a great deal about our personal history and social identity through the way we speak.

What are the factors that define a person's identity? When you think of your identity, do you think of yourself in *relation* to someone else? For example, do you think of yourself as someone's daughter or wife, or someone's father or brother?

Perhaps you see identity in terms of *membership* of a particular *group*? If so, how large a group is it? Is it a national group? An ethnic group? A social group? An interest group? A family group?

When members of a group are together for a common purpose, they feel a sense of belonging, of being united, and a sense of having a shared experience. 'Identity' in this context means 'belonging to the group'. This sense of unity and identity is often demonstrated by the *language* used by the members of the group, and by the particular *choice* of language used to express this identity.

The following summary outlines some of the most important notions to bear in mind as you think about questions of language and identity:

- *geographic identity*   a sense of belonging to an area or to the people of a region or place one was born in
- *ethnic identity*   allegiance to a group with which one has ancestral links
- *personal identity*   a sense of belonging to a peer group (with a certain kind of education, occupation, age, sex, and personality)
- *national identity*   a sense of belonging to a larger group, a 'nation', or a state
- *social identity*   a sense of belonging to a social 'class'. (The notion of 'class' is subjective and controversial.)

- *social solidarity*   the desire to associate and identify with a certain group
- *social distance*   the desire to separate oneself from a certain group

If you think about this topic, you will probably realize that you cannot define your identity in terms of one of these aspects only. You will realize that there are many sides or facets to your identity, just as there are many facets to a cut diamond.

Activity 1   Your own identity

We would like you to consider the many facets of your identity as a way of starting to think about your own linguistic identity. Draw a mind-map as a way of expressing these facets. Write your own name in the space at the centre of the mind-map, and then, branching off from this, write down as many aspects of your identity as you can think of: your various *relationships*, the *groups* to which you belong, and the different *situations* in which you operate.

Then, when you have written down as many aspects of your identity as you can think of, write down the *language* or *variety* of language you use in each of the groups, relationships, or situations you find yourself in.

IDIOLECT

It is very revealing to hear your speech being imitated or repeated by your own children or by a group of learners in an educational situation. You then realize which words or phrases you repeat most often. These words and phrases have become a sort of 'signature tune': they are associated with you and almost serve to identify you. They are part of your *idiolect*.

An 'idiolect' is a person's personal dialect; their individual speech habits. Your idiolect consists of your word choice (lexical choice), your choice of particular grammatical constructions, and the way you pronounce your words (phonology), as well as your accent.

An example of a *grammatical* idiolect feature would be found in the *constructions* that a particular person uses often. In your daily encounters with people, try to raise your awareness of these personal habits. In some people, distinctive speech features are more obvious than in others. Someone we know intersperses all his spoken sentences with 'Do you follow?' Some eager listeners may respond to everything they hear with 'Cool!' or 'Great!' Someone else may often use the construction: '... the reason being, is that ...'

Another acquaintance, who happens to be a teacher, numbers everything he says as though he is relating a list of points: 'I decided to move out of town. One: my car was broken into twice. Two: things never quietened down at night, and I wasn't sleeping well. Three: ...' Every story he tells is structured like a lecture delivered for the benefit of students taking notes. This is an example of a grammatical construction that is characteristic of a person's occupation as well as their idiolect.

An example of a *lexical* idiolect feature would be found in the words that a particular person uses repeatedly. Learners soon come to recognize the words favoured by their teachers and regard these words as characteristic of them, sometimes even repeating them jokingly after the teacher has used them.

Activity 2 Your own idiolect

We would now like you to start analysing your own characteristic English idiolect. Even if English is not your primary language (the first language you learned as a child), you will probably have got into the habit of using certain English words and phrases more than others.

For this activity, you could simply list the words, phrases, and expressions that you feel are characteristic of you and your spoken English. You could start by becoming aware of your use of particular *adjectives*, for example. The adjectives we use very often express our attitudes and feelings about many things and events, and are therefore sometimes quite distinctive (in other words, they are easily recognizable).

You could also take note of any *colloquialisms* (remember that 'colloquialisms' are spoken words and expressions used in informal situations), *idiomatic expressions*, and even *proverbs* that you are fond of and that you find you use often.

INDIVIDUAL SPEECH FEATURES

We would now like to link the topics we have discussed in this chapter so far: the question of *identity*, and the question of *idiolect*. What is the connection between the two?

We suggested earlier that a person's identity can be defined partly by the groups and relationships to which they belong. These groups and relationships also help to shape the way in which that person uses language. This is especially true of the primary language a person learns from birth, but it is also true of additional languages learned later.

We do not suggest that there is a definite one-to-one relationship between a person's way of speaking and their identity. Nor do we suggest that one is *caused* by the other. You cannot say that a member of a particular group will *definitely* speak in a particular way. Nor can you say that a person who speaks in a particular way does so *because* he or she belongs to a particular group. For the moment, we would simply like you to be aware that some sort of relationship exists between the two.

We focus here on four aspects of a person's identity that may be indicated or revealed by their specific use of language: the *region* from which they come, their *gender*, their *age*, and their *social position*. We are limiting ourselves to English specifically, but suggest that you do the same with any other languages with which you are familiar.

Before we consider how these factors may influence English usage in South Africa specifically, we would like to remind you that you can use the three aspects of language usage we mentioned on page 33 in Chapter 2 when you examine language as an indicator of identity:

Word choice
(lexis or vocabulary)

a person's choice of particular *words* may provide a clue to their identity. (We are going to use the word *lexis* from now on in this section.)

Syntax

choice of *sentence structure* and combinations of words within sentences provide clues.

Phonology
(the way you *sound*)

pronunciation, *accent*, and *intonation* (which includes *volume*, *pitch*, and *stress patterns*) all help to identify a person.

Let us now return to *region*, *gender*, *age*, and *social position* as aspects of identity.

Region

When you hear someone from Britain speaking English, it is sometimes possible to work out what geographic *region* or area they come from, using clues such as their *pronunciation, lexis,* and *grammar.* You can often tell the difference, say, between the speech of someone from Scotland and someone from London.

This was especially true in the past, when it was much easier to identify the origin of a person. Today it is more difficult to identify someone's origin, because people tend to move around far more than they used to. Today it is rare for people to be born, to live, and to die in the same district. Greater exposure to different accents on radio and television also influences our accents and pronunciation.

What is the situation in South Africa? Can you tell the difference, say, between the spoken English of someone from Cape Town or Durban, and someone from Gauteng? There are people who maintain that there are very noticeable differences between the spoken English of people from these regions.

However, it is our view that mother-tongue or primary language influences, rather than regional influences, have the greater effect on the way South Africans speak English. Primary-language speakers of Afrikaans will speak English differently from primary-language speakers of an indigenous African language. This point was made in Chapter 1 by William Branford, whom we quote below. For 'L1', read PL (primary language) and for 'L2' read AL (additional language):

> English and its varieties in South Africa have furthermore, an identificatory or 'demarcating' role. Through the selection of one language over another or of one variety of the same language over another, speakers display 'acts of identity'. For South African speakers of English as L2, important signals of identity are often made by the 'pull' of their L1 upon their English.[1]

We can all think of South Africans we know whose use of English illustrates the 'pull' of their primary language. You can probably call to mind specific examples of expressions used by additional-language speakers of English. You may wish to refer to the South African examples of non-standard English we listed on page 80 in Chapter 4, under the heading 'How much deviation should be tolerated?'

Gender

Our sex definitely affects the way we speak. In some languages, males and females use different pronunciation, grammar, and lexis. In English, male and female speakers use the same grammatical forms, words, and patterns of pronunciation, but there may be differences in the *frequency* with which they use them. They also display different speech habits, some examples of which follow.

Studies[2] show that women tend to use more emotive language than men, and tend to make more use of exclamations such as *'Goodness!'* Women also use more intensifiers (*so* and *such*) as in 'It was *such* a busy day' and 'I am *so* tired'. Studies show that women also tend to speak more 'correctly' than men and use fewer non-standard features in their speech.

Men tend to swear more than women, and use slang more frequently. In conversation they are less polite and interrupt more than women do. Women offer more support and encouragement to those they are talking to: they ask more questions and are more responsive listeners than are men. Men are more assertive in their speech than women, but are likely to ignore what has been said, or dispute the points made by others.

Speech differences between men and women tend to reflect their different traditional social roles. Men have been conditioned to be more dominant, while women have been conditioned to play a more supportive role. When women ask questions in a group, they tend to give others the chance to express themselves, while perhaps suppressing their own need for expression. In terms of social expectations, a degree of aggression is acceptable in men but often disapproved of in women. It is regarded as normal for men to challenge the views of others, but it is less acceptable when women do so.

However, we do not want to fall into the trap of stereotyping. We need to be cautious when we talk in general terms about 'men' and 'women'. Neither category is homogenous, and each includes enormous differences between individuals. For the moment, we would simply like you to be aware of these suggested differences in the different use of English by males and females. Observe male and female interaction in conversational situations, and see whether you can recognize the contrasts we have described. We would also like you to consider the point made about other languages. Do you know any languages that use different pronunciation, grammar, and lexis for males and females?

Age

The main distinguishing feature between people of different age groups is *lexis* or word choice, especially informal lexis or colloquialisms. Very often, people use particular colloquialisms in their youth, and go on using them throughout their adult lives.

It would be relatively easy to draw up a list of colloquialisms used by members of particular age groups. You could start by listening to the speech of teenagers, taking note of their favourite words and expressions. It might be interesting to note which ones have been picked up from American television. You could then compare these with colloquialisms used by people born just after the Second World War, who would now be in their late fifties or early sixties. Perhaps you would find the most distinctive examples among primary-language speakers of English.

It would be interesting to combine the two aspects of region and age and see what South African examples you can identify. For example, we suspect that the word *bioscope* is used only by South African English speakers of a certain age (forty years and older).

Although we have focused on *lexis* so far, there is one current example of teenagers' speech involving *grammar* that is particularly distinctive. Look at the sentence below, spoken by a South African teenager:

'She said she was going to that club, so then *I'm like*: "Why do you want to go there? It's boring."'

In introducing a quotation, as in the example, some teenagers use the grammatical construction 'I'm like …' instead of the usual 'I said …' Listen carefully to American movies or television programmes, or to teenagers themselves in conversation, and you are likely to pick this up.

Another example, this time relating to *phonology* (pronunciation), is the way young people pronounce the phrase '*as* well ', as though it is one word, and with the accent on the word *as*. We first became aware of this change in the early '90s, when, instead of saying: 'I wore a jersey, a jacket, and a scarf as well ', teenagers would say: 'I wore a jersey, a jacket, and a scarf *as*well', or: 'I had a bad cold, a sore throat, and a terrible cough *as*well'.

In time, this linguistic idiosyncrasy will function as a marker of age: you will be able to date people according to how they pronounce 'as well'. If they pronounce 'as well' as two words with equal stress, they may have grown up before the 1990s: if they stress *as* more than *well*, they are likely to be younger.

Why this kind of change takes place it is impossible to say, but it illustrates the point made in Chapter 2: namely, that language is dynamic and constantly undergoes change.

Social position

This refers to the status or position of a group within a social hierarchy. We can talk about somebody belonging to the 'upper class', the 'middle class' or the 'lower class'. However, as we have mentioned before, the notion of *class* is very controversial. Are there clear-cut levels in society? If we accept that there are, how does one determine to which 'class' somebody belongs? What are the factors that make us decide this? What criteria do we use? Which of the following factors would you consider relevant if you were to assess your own social 'class'?

- where you live
- the way you dress
- the way you speak
- your manners and mannerisms
- how much money you have
- your family background
- which school you attended
- your level of education
- the kind of work you do
- the hobbies and interests you have

There are no simple answers to the questions surrounding the notion of social status. Human beings and society are so complex that it is impossible to pigeonhole people neatly into 'classes'; nor are there fixed social strata. Not only can the social status of people change radically in the course of their lifetimes, but people play multiple roles during their lives, and their status in different roles may vary enormously. It is impossible to define social position exactly, and any attempts to classify people according to 'class' should be regarded with caution and sensitivity.

However, it is also true that we all make value judgements about the people we meet in everyday life. In any social situation there is a great deal of 'sizing up' going on: we form impressions and try to assess one another's social status on the basis of largely unexamined values. Most people would agree that economic position, level of education and the way people talk do have something to do with the perception of social position or 'class'. For our purpose, *use of language* is of course the factor that most interests us.

There was a time in Britain when the way you spoke could mark you immediately as a member of a particular 'class', and could cause you to be treated in a particular way. You may be familiar with the film *My Fair Lady* (based on the play *Pygmalion* by George Bernard Shaw) where a young, 'lower-class' flower-seller is taken off the streets and trained in 'upper-class' speech and behaviour by a professor of language. It is significant that the focus of this education process is her use of English. The ultimate 'test' she has to pass is a speech test to prove she is able to speak with the 'refined' accent, register, and style of English high society. Some people would argue that little has changed in this regard, and that speech is still the great determining factor of social position.

In our opinion, the traditional idea of 'class' may not be as clearly defined an indicator of social identity in South Africa as it may be in Britain. We also feel that, in a multilingual society such as South Africa, class is not indicated to the same extent by the way in which a person speaks English, which is only one of its languages.

In South Africa, the context in which children learned English (known as the *acquisitional context*) was influenced almost entirely by their race until recently, because each race was represented by a separate educational department. Today, the context in which children learn has opened up a great deal. Where they live and which languages are commonly used in their regions and at school will influence the way they speak English. Additionally, children are exposed to different languages and varieties of English on radio and television, which are also important factors in their English acquisitional context.

SOUTH AFRICAN ENGLISH VARIETIES

Is there such a thing as a variety of South African English? South African English speakers are often instantly recognizable to speakers of English from other parts of the world. In this section, we would like you to consider what aspects of English usage identify someone as a speaker of South African English.

We would like to look first at *lexis* as a possible marker of South African national language identity. For example, South Africans use the word *robot* to indicate a set of traffic lights. They are probably the only English speakers in the world who do so. Other common examples of South African lexis are *braai* and *veld*.

Which word do *you* use to describe those crisp, wafer-thin pieces of potato, deep-fried in oil and sold in sealed foil packets? Are they *chips* or *crisps*? And if they are *chips*, how do you distinguish them from those long rectangular pieces of potato (also deep-fried in oil) that are sold at fast-food outlets and sometimes accompany hamburgers or fried fish? Are they *chips* or '*slap*' *chips*?

What about the exclamation '*Shame!*'? It is not a uniquely South African word, but it can be used in a uniquely South African way. The word actually denotes a negative feeling (look it up in your dictionary), but many South Africans use it to express sympathy in certain situations. Where else in the world would you hear the expression '*Sis!*' used to express disgust?

When asking for confirmation of something that has been said, some South Africans may say 'Is it?' instead of 'Is that so?' In England, you may be asked 'Is that right?' It is doubtful that you will hear the question 'Is it?' used in this way elsewhere in the world.

The article below appeared in the *Mail & Guardian* of 6 to 12 August 1999, and is an excerpt from an editorial comment on the tenth edition of the *Concise Oxford Dictionary*. The writer points out that this dictionary contains words that are regarded as South African English.[3]

THE 10TH EDITION of the *Concise Oxford Dictionary*, released in South Africa this week, contains many new words, including a selection from South Africa.

English has always been an absorptive language, building itself, over the centuries, from Old Germanic, Anglo-Saxon, French, Latin, Greek and other tongues. The vast colonial empire of the British ensured that it colonised words as well, bringing *veld*, *khaki*, *rajah* and many others into the language. Today, as English expands into ever more of a global *lingua franca*, so it absorbs words from other languages and from slang.

South African words in the new Concise Oxford include *baas*, *bundu*, *dwaal*, *eina*, *hamba*, *lekker*, *predikant*, *sommer*, *toyi-toyi*, *tricameral*, *veldskoen* and *wors*.

It's good to see South African English (of whatever hybrid of English and other languages it is we actually speak) acknowledged in so august a publication.

One does, however, wonder about a couple of these additions. A secondary meaning of *veldskoen* (not *velskoen*, note), as a modifier, is given as 'conservative or reactionary'. I can't find anyone who's heard of that usage.

And it might have been enlightening to explain that *dwaal*, n. ('dreamy, dazed or absent-minded state') comes from the Afrikaans verb meaning to wander.

Mail & Guardian, 6–12 August, 1999

Apart from distinctively South African items of vocabulary (discussed above), we are sure you would agree that there is a distinctively South African English accent (or varieties of accent).

We would like to remind you that *dialect* and *accent* are two different things. *Accent* refers only to distinctive pronunciation, whereas *dialect* refers to distinctive pronunciation, grammar, and vocabulary (refer to Chapter 2).

Remember, when talking about accent, to avoid taking a prescriptive position and assuming that some accents are 'better' than others. English spoken with a particular regional accent is not inferior; merely different. It is perfectly possible to speak good, standard English with a strong regional accent. People who react critically to this assertion need to examine, and try to overcome, their own prejudices.

Here now is a discussion of features of a South African dialect, slightly adapted from an editorial in the *Pretoria News*:

Howzit uitlander, here's how to gooi the taal on your visit

HOWZIT! Jislaaik! Lekker, ag shame! Eina and bioscope. Donder and skinder.

Words that are all part of a unique South African *patois*, well-known to most of the indigenous folk who live here. They're colourful, naive and peppered with humour. They're an integral part of the South African lexicon, an indelible feature of the social landscape.

A list entitled *A Survival Guide for Visitors to South Africa* explains some of these terms for uninitiated uitlanders (foreigners). Here's a sample.

'Ag shame!' Like 'No', 'shame' can mean the opposite of its meaning in other parts of the world. If someone shows you a baby, you can say 'Ag shame'. This does not mean the baby is ugly, it means the baby is cute.

If the baby is ugly, it is more appropriate to say 'Shame hey!' If the baby is truly hideous, it is appropriate to say 'Jislaaik!' Don't be surprised if this does not receive a warm welcome from the baby's parents.

'Izit?' An essential word in South Africanese. Derived from the two words 'is' and 'it', it can be used when you have nothing to contribute to the conversation. If someone tells you at the braai: 'The Russians will succeed in their bid for capitalism once they adopt a work ethic and respect for private ownership', it is appropriate to respond by saying: 'Izit?'

Jislaaik! Pronounced Yis-laaik, this is an interjection conveying astonishment. For instance, if someone tells you there are 1 billion people in China, a suitable comment would be 'Jislaaik, that's a hang of a lot of people, hey!'

Jawellnofine. This is another conversation fall-back word. Derived from the four words yes, well, no and fine, it means roughly 'How about that!' If your bank manager tells you your account is overdrawn, you can say with confidence 'jawellnofine'.

Just now. Universally used, it means very recently, eventually and sometimes never. It never means now this minute. For instance, if someone says he will do something just now, it could be in ten minutes or tomorrow, or maybe he won't do it at all.

Now-now. From the Afrikaans nou-nou, it means just now.

Lekker. An Afrikaans word meaning nice, this word is used by all language groups to express approval. If you see someone who is sexy, you can exclaim 'Lekkerrr!' while drawing out the last syllable. But that use is now thought politically incorrect in some circles.

Lappie is a cloth or rag used to wipe up a mess. You will find it in a machine shop to clean up oil spills, or in the nursery to wipe up baby food. Sometimes also called a jammer lappie (sorry cloth).

Donner. A rude word which comes from the Afrikaans, donder (thunder). Pronounced dorner, it means beat up. Your rugby team can get donnered in a game or your boss can donner you if you do a lousy job.

With. A preposition used by most South Africans without being followed by a noun or pronoun. For example, you can ask your friend 'Are you coming with to the bioscope?'

Arguably, words like these have enriched the English language and become part of our collective unconscious. What would our conversation be without them?

Pretoria News, 24 May, 2001

Activity 3 South African dialects

Reread the article 'Howzit Uitlander…' then answer the questions that follow.
1   In Britain, the phrase 'just now' means 'at the moment' or 'a moment ago'. These are examples of its usage in that country:

'Would you like some tea?'
'Not just now, thank you.'
'I bumped into a friend as I was crossing the street just now.'
What, according to the editorial, would confuse a British English speaker about the way South Africans use the phrase 'just now'?

2 Would you say that the writer of this article has a *prescriptive* or *descriptive* approach to language?

3 Justify the answer you gave in question 2.

4 Rewrite the following dialogue, using *standard English*.
  A: We're going to Joburg now now.
  B: Is it?
  A: Ja! D'ja wanna come with?

The dialect we have just been reading about in the *Pretoria News* article is recognizably a 'white' South African dialect, spoken by people who have close connections with Afrikaans. In Chapter 2 we looked at the use of a 'Coloured' dialect in the poem 'Da same, da same'. So-called Black dialects of English also exist. One of these is *Iscamtho*, an urban dialect influenced by the Nguni languages, found in certain townships, and spoken mainly by young people.[4]

Knowing *Iscamtho* gains instant acceptance and respect among these young people, and means you're part of the 'grassroots'. (This perception is linked closely with our discussion of 'language and identity' earlier in this chapter. Using this particular dialect is a way of showing *social solidarity* with others in the group. It would also be a way of keeping a *social distance* from those who do not belong to the 'in-group'.) Depending on how you speak, the young men in the group, the guys (*amagents*) can tell if you're streetwise or are *i-kom ver*, a word derived from Afrikaans meaning that he or she comes from afar. An *i-kom ver* could be from the Transkei, KwaZulu-Natal, Maputo, or even New York. An *i-kom ver* could also have returned from exile.

Some examples of the innovative and vibrant dialect of *Iscamtho* follow:

Communicating in Kwaito

LIKE ALL SUBCULTURES — the Beat generation, the hippies, the Ivys — kwaito fans speak a language of their own. The language is *Iscamtho*, a combination of English, Afrikaans and African languages, but not readily recognisable to a purist speaker of any of those languages. Here are some *Iscamtho* words that you can hear on YFM or on the streets:

A nip of brandy	*icellphone*
It's nice	*kumnca*
It's okay	*sharp-sharp*
Truth	*ivara*
BMW cabriolet	*is'lahla*
white person	*ilarnie; ungamla*
Fool	*moegoe; bhari; mampara*
To flee	*to space*
Trouble	*ismoko*
Knife	*igoni*
Two rand coin	*uDe Klerk*
Ten rand note	*itiger*
R5 coin	*ihalf tiger*
R20 note	*itwo tiger, ichockie*
R50 note	*ipinkie*
Car	*ikara; smuvana*
Girlfriend	*i18; ithekeni*
Music	*igongo*
Party	*ivibe; umcimbi*
Sex	*inkauza; umdavaso; tseva; fathaza*
Food	*iguage; igaula*
Gun	*ingadla; lagaza*
Home	*iplek; ipozzy; iplaas*

Sunday Times, August 9, 1998

These examples obviously focus on the *lexis* of *Iscamtho*. It is interesting to see how new words are formed by combining English, Afrikaans, and African languages. The word 'cellphone' is the same as the English except for the prefix *i*, in keeping with the grammatical requirements of the Nguni group of languages, but in *Iscamtho* it means something quite different from a cellular telephone; namely 'a nip of brandy'. The use of this word would be totally misleading to somebody unfamiliar with this dialect. The word *ivara* ('it's true') is formed from the Afrikaans word *waar* (meaning 'true'), given an English phonetic spelling, and then pre-fixed with the Nguni *i*.

So much for the lexis of *Iscamtho*. We should also consider the *syntax* of the dialect. Here is a piece of continuous prose. It is part of an article in which the writer has deliberately used elements of *Iscamtho* for humorous effect:

GA! NAGQIBELA ngo Noah when apartheid forbade the so-called Kweres who were forbidden to come to South Africa, mtshana. This is a new South Africa mtshana, where the Kweres are free to come and go, xeno-phobia notwithstanding. And, manje, mtshana, the Kweres are here big time. They are even making fly darkie laaities van Jozi look like plaas-japies, ek sê jou tsharo.

After all, the so-called Kweres came and stole Hillbrow right under the noses of volle clevers van Mjibha, mtshana. And to prove that hulle is "clevers tussen clevers", as the jita lingo goes, they've got the local mlungu cherries, nogal, dancing to their music. Ja, Jack, the same mlungu cherries the clevers used to call "die klein maddie", during those apartheid days, or "madam", "miesies" en "baas", are now calling the moegoe Makwankwis die baas. Yeah it's happening right in Hillbrow, mtshana, where the drug-addicted larnie cherries work for the Kwere drug dealers.

And the Kwere moegoes have coolly walked into the so-called "clever se toun" and taken over without even paying any dues to the ouens! Huh, how's that for spunk, mtshana?

Joe Khumalo (award-winning journalist), *Pace Magazine*, 1999

Activity 4 'Yeah mtshana …'

1 Consider the non-standard features of the language used in the article by Joe Khumalo. Try to find examples from the three branches of language study: *syntax (sentence structure)*, *lexis*, and *phonology*.

2 Imagine how a person from the UK, the USA, or Australia would respond to this dialect. Do you think it would be intelligible to them?

3 On reading the above article, what argument could be made for using 'standard' English?

(Compare your answers with those we suggest at the end of the book.)

SUMMARY

We would like to summarize the main points of this chapter:

- An individual's use of language reveals a great deal about individual identity.
- There are many different factors that shape personal identities and the individual's use of language.
- People express different aspects of their identity by varying their use of language according to each situation they find themselves in.
- Individual speech habits are known as idiolects.
- Several different dialects are spoken in South Africa. These are strongly influenced by the primary languages of the speakers.
- Dialect and accent are two different things.
- The non-standard features of some South African dialects are extreme and would not be intelligible to English speakers in other parts of the world.

GLOSSARY

Here is a list of some important terms used in this chapter. Fill in the missing definitions, and add other terms and definitions.

idiolect   a person's personal dialect and their individual speech habits

dialect   a particular variety of a language in which the non-standard lexis, syntax and phonology identify the speaker's regional and social background

ethnic identity _____

_____

national identity _____

_____

social identity _____

_____

social solidarity _____

_____

social distance _____

_____

ENDNOTES

1 BRANFORD, WILLIAM. 1996. 'English in South African society: a preliminary overview' in Vivian de Klerk, ed. *Focus on South Africa*, p. 36. Amsterdam: John Benjamins.

2 For those of you who may be interested in pursuing this fascinating comparison of the speech of men and women, there are a number of books on the subject you could explore. One example is *Girls, boys and language*, by Joan Swann. 1992. Oxford: Blackwell.

3 There are a number of dictionaries available that deal specifically with South African English usage. For example, the *South African Concise Oxford Dictionary*. 2002. Cape Town: Oxford University Press.

Other less recent ones include: BRANFORD, JEAN. 1991. *A Dictionary of South African English*. Cape Town: Oxford University Press.
SILVA, PENNY. 1996. *A Dictionary of South African English on Historical Principles*. Oxford: Oxford University Press.

4 There is a programme broadcast on Radio SAFM every Sunday morning at 08:30, called 'Word of mouth'. Language issues, and particularly those relating to South African English usage, are discussed by language experts. You may find it interesting to tune in and listen to discussion on the sort of topics we deal with in this chapter.

6 Is spoken language different from written language?

CHAPTER OUTLINE

We now turn to a discussion of the characteristics of spoken and written language, and the relationship between them. We also consider the nature of conversation and how culture influences the 'rules' of such interaction.

LEARNING OUTCOMES

By the end of this chapter you should have the following knowledge, skills, values, and attitudes:

Knowledge

You should understand
- that speech pre-dates written language
- that spoken language has different characteristics from written language
- that attitudes towards speech and writing differ
- the interactive nature of conversation
- the factors that contribute towards success in conversation, and
- how cultural factors influence the rules of conversation.

Skills

You should be able
- to tabulate the information in a given text
- to describe the factors that influence conversational success
- to analyse conversational turn-taking and exchanges, and
- to recognize implicatures in conversation.

Values and attitudes

You should develop
- a recognition of the value and importance of the spoken and written forms of language for different purposes, and
- sensitivity to, and respect for, the cultural differences that underlie the rules of conversation.

INTRODUCTION

Speech is the primary medium of language, and it developed well before writing. Of course we cannot know with any certainty how long human-kind has been talking, but spoken language pre-dates written language by a long time. Writing based on alphabetic script is a relatively recent development, only a few thousand years old. In fact, many languages used in the world today still do not have written form.

Speech is the production of sequences of sounds by allowing air from the lungs to pass up and out through the mouth and nose. The vocal tracts of human beings have evolved in such a way that the highly sophisticated process of speech is possible. In Hayakawa's words:

> ... [H]uman beings use extremely complicated systems of sputtering, hissing, gurgling, clucking, cooing noises called language, with which they express and report what goes on in their nervous systems.[1]

When we speak, we produce a stream of noises that can be broken down into separate sounds. These are combined in an infinite number of ways to convey different meanings. Each meaning-specific sound in a language is described as a *phoneme*. The study of the characteristics of speech sounds is called *phonetics*. *Articulatory phonetics* is the study of how speech sounds are made, or articulated. *Phonology* is the description of the systems and patterns of speech sounds in a language.

Oral communication between human beings is, by definition, transient – it does not last, or certainly did not before modern technology made it possible to capture sounds on tapes and other devices. The need for a more permanent, stable record of information probably motivated the development of writing. Hayakawa describes the evolution of writing in the following way:

In addition to having developed language, man has also developed means of making, on clay tablets, bits of wood or stone, skins of animals, and paper, more or less permanent marks and scratches which *stand* for language. These marks enable him to communicate with people who are beyond the reach of his voice both in space and time. There is a long course of evolution from the marked trees that indicated Indian trails to the metropolitan daily newspaper, but they have this in common: they pass on what one individual has known to other individuals, for their convenience or instruction.[2]

Hayakawa stresses the incalculable advantages of the *permanence* of the written form of language to the human race:

Archimedes is dead, but we still have his reports on what he observed in his experiments. Keats is dead, but he can still tell us how he felt on first reading Chapman's Homer ... The cultural accomplishments of the ages, the invention of cooking, of weapons, of writing, of printing, of building, of methods of building, of games and amusements, of means of transportation, and the discoveries of all the arts and sciences come to as *free gifts from the dead* ... To be able to read and write, therefore, is to learn to profit by and take part in the greatest human achievements – namely the pooling of our experiences in great co-operative stores of knowledge, available to all.[3]

Describing the writings of the past as *free gifts from the dead* is, we're sure you will agree, a striking way of expressing the value of the written word, and how much richer it can make our lives. By means of writing, we have access to some of the finest minds of all time.

ATTITUDES TOWARDS SPEECH AND WRITING

Linguists and people interested in language study have different *attitudes* towards spoken and written language. Speech and writing have at various times been seen to be in competition with one another, with either one or the other being regarded as a more valuable and worthwhile object of study.[4]

In the past, written language was regarded as *superior* to spoken language for several reasons. First of all, it was regarded as a reference source of *standards* of linguistic excellence because it was the medium of literature. The act of writing language down gave it *permanence* and *authority*. Written texts were used to illustrate the 'rules' of grammar. It was felt that spoken language, on the other hand, lacked 'care', 'organization' and 'rules'.

The backlash to this attitude came in the twentieth century. It was felt that speech, not writing, should be the object of language study. The following reasons were given for this approach:

- speech is older than writing
- children learn to speak before they learn to write
- writing systems are based on the sounds of speech
- speech is the primary medium of communication among all people, and
- some languages have never been written down at all.

However, none of these reasons fully justifies why the study of speech should replace the study of writing. Instead, there needs to be a compromise. Neither speech nor writing can be regarded as a *substitute* for the other: both are valuable and necessary. Each fulfils certain specific needs in specific contexts, and each complements the other.

DIFFERENCES BETWEEN SPEECH AND WRITING

Speech and writing can be seen as alternative but equal 'systems of linguistic expression'. The word 'alternative' suggests that these two systems may be used for different *purposes*. We will come back to the issue of purpose once we have looked in greater detail at the differences between speech and writing.

The most obvious difference between speech and writing is that of *physical form*: the substance of speech is 'phonic' (sound, caused by air-pressure movements in the vocal tract), whereas the substance of writing is 'graphic' (visual marks on a surface). However, the more interesting differences are those of *structure* and *use*. We will return to a comparison of structure and use shortly.

THE CHARACTERISTICS OF SPEECH

The average person's speech is marked by 'non-fluency features'. This means that most people do *not* speak fluently: their speech is character-ized by pauses, hesitations, and expressions like '*you know*' and '*umm*'. These are called 'fillers', because they literally fill the gaps in the stream of language and slow down speech in order to provide thinking time. Noises like '*uh*' and '*er*' are known as 'voiced pauses' – the speaker 'buys time' in order to think of what to say next.

Other non-fluency features include 'false starts', when a speaker begins to say something, then decides to rephrase it: '*It looks to me ... I mean it stands to reason that ...*', and repetition, when a phrase or word is said more than once to give the speaker more time to think. Speakers often go back to put in something they should have said before: '*... so I went to the chemist to get the medicine, but it was closed ... oh yes – by the way – I forgot to mention it was a public holiday ...*'

All speech is characterized by non-fluency features, which naturally result from the spontaneity of speech: we make up what we are going to say as we go along. Of course there is spoken language that is not spontaneous. When a politician addresses an audience at a political rally, or the minister of finance delivers his budget speech in parliament, these are carefully planned and thought out down to the last detail. This type of speech is not typical of natural speech and shares more of the features of written language.

A COMPARISON OF SPEECH AND WRITING

Talking does not conform to the same rules as writing. As we have mentioned, speech is usually much more spontaneous than writing. We do not always speak in complete sentences, for example, but no one would think of correcting a speaker by saying: '*What you have just said is not a complete sentence*'. (This would be an example of a prescriptive approach, and treating spoken English as though it were standard written English). Speech, by its very nature, is much more 'loose' and informal than writing.

Speech is transient and dynamic, whereas writing is more deliberate, permanent, and static in nature. Written English is usually the standard form so that it can be understood by all readers, whereas spoken language is adapted to a particular audience at a particular moment, and commonly includes a number of non-standard features.

Because writing is permanent, it tends to have a higher status than spoken language. Legal contracts, for example, have to be in writing to be fully binding. Sacred material is often written down (for example the Bible and the Koran). In many languages the written word carries more weight and authority than the spoken word.

However, there are certain examples of spoken language that do have special ceremonial power and meaning in religious and other formal contexts, for example the words: '*I do therefore pronounce you man and wife*'. (We referred to this *performative* function of language in Chapter 3.)

In speech, both speaker(s) and listener(s) are present and can be easily identified, whereas in writing the writer is distant from the reader(s), and the writer cannot be certain of who the readers are. In a written interaction where the parties are not physically together, the writer cannot use the context to clarify what he or she has to say. Therefore, writers have to be far more thorough and careful to communicate clearly, than speakers need to be. Speakers can rely on gestures and other *paralinguistic features* (for example body language, gestures, and facial expressions) to aid communication, and can see for themselves whether the listener(s) follow their speech. In the written form of language, there is usually no immediate feedback as there is during conversation.

Written language can use typographical features such as capital letters, subheadings, and paragraphing to indicate the structure and organization of the material, but spoken language cannot convey structure nearly as clearly. Volume, expression, and emphasis can help to get the spoken message across, but may not be precise.

Activity 1 Differences between speech and writing

We would now like you to summarize the above information. Fill in the gaps in the table below.

Speech	Writing
Substance	**Substance** The substance is graphic (visual marks on a surface).
Time Speech is usually time-bound and transient (impermanent).	**Time**
Space	**Space** Writing is space-bound (the producer is distant from the recipient).
Planning With the exception of prepared speeches, spoken language is usually spontaneous and is not planned in advance.	**Planning**
Division into units	**Division into units** Division can be indicated by means of layout, design, and punctuation.
Context	**Context** As participants cannot see one another, they cannot rely on the context and feedback to make meaning clear.

Contrasts Some contrasts cannot be conveyed in speech, but changes in volume and pitch of the voice can draw attention to contrasts.	**Contrasts**
Grammar and lexis Colloquial words and expressions are commonly used and regarded as acceptable. Sentences are often incomplete and change as the conversation goes along. Many non-standard features may be present.	**Grammar and lexis**
Formality	**Formality** Written language tends to be more formal than speech.
Special uses Spoken language is used less often than writing for special purposes. (However, special forms of spoken language are set aside for ceremonial or religious occasions.)	**Special uses**

Activity 2 Your own speech and writing

Reflect on your own use of speech and writing. Which system do you think you use more? For what purposes do you use speech? For what purposes do you use writing?

ADVANTAGES OF BOTH

As indicated above, both systems of language (speech and writing) have advantages for different purposes. Modern society has evolved different uses for these two systems.

Give some thought to the ways in which these two systems overlap or sometimes replace one another. For example, is a 'chat room' on the Internet an example of the use of speech or writing? The messages people send one another obviously have a written form, but people definitely seem to write as they speak, without paying very much attention to spelling, punctuation, and layout, for example. Their messages are transient (not permanent unless stored or printed), and are interactive in that they rely to a large extent on the immediate situation (on immediate transfer), and on immediate response. They also make use of visual signals or icons to convey emotion (called 'emoticons'), much as one makes use of facial expression in face-to-face conversation. It is also possible to convey volume: 'shouting' is indicated by capital letters and a bold font.

Here are two examples of the emoticons people use when communicating via the computer:

:)   This is meant to be interpreted as a smiling face (viewed sideways) to convey positive emotion.

:(This suggests sadness or displeasure.

There are many more examples of emoticons, and more are being developed and used all the time.

SPEECH AND SUCCESS IN CONVERSATION

We have discussed the relationship between speech and writing, and various attitudes towards them as objects of language study. We now consider the structure of conversation. What is it that makes a conversation 'successful' or 'unsuccessful'?

Conversations constantly take place in everyday life and are spontaneous and unplanned. Therefore, they may be thought to be completely random and unstructured. However, this is not so. Conversations follow certain patterns and unwritten 'rules', for example: who speaks, when, and for how long. We gradually learn these rules and conventions through socialization. Every society has its own conventions, and rules differ from culture to culture.

Participants in a conversation are not consciously aware of the 'rules', but when someone breaks them, people can sense immediately that something has gone wrong. When the participants go against the usual conventions, conversations can quickly degenerate into chaos, with people not listening to one another and perhaps talking simultaneously. Frustration and irritation are the result of such conversational break-downs. Conversations that 'fail' in this way demonstrate that the 'rules' have not been observed, and highlight the reality that successful conversational behaviour is systematic, highly organized, and requires definite skills. A conversation may be regarded as successful if it is smooth, and proceeds according to the expectations of the participants.

The success of a conversation may be judged according to different rules in different cultures. In our multilingual and multicultural South African society, it is useful, and indeed respectful, to find out what rules for conversation apply in the culture of the people with whom one is conversing. Read the following simple dialogue, which illustrates how different values operate in a cross-cultural exchange:

Setting: Sipho knocks at Denis' office door.

DENIS: *Good morning Sipho, can I help?*

SIPHO: *Mr Venter, good morning. How are you Mr Venter?*

DENIS: *I am well thank you Sipho. What is it?*

SIPHO: *Mr Venter, we have been talking and we have decided that you are a good man.*

DENIS: *Well, thank you Sipho. Can you please tell me now why you have come to see me because I still have much to do before the board meeting starts at ten o'clock, and it is important that I am well-prepared.*

SIPHO: *Yes, Mr Venter ...*[5]

This exchange illustrates the difference in attitude towards time and what constitutes polite behaviour between Western and African people. The Westerner believes that every minute counts, and time should not be wasted on things that appear to have no relevance. The Western person is not really interested in what he perceives to be the 'small talk' that precedes the real topic. The African, on the other hand, comes from a human-centred culture, in which it is bad manners to consider work as more important than human relations. He therefore tries to create the right climate and waits for a conversational 'sign' from his 'superior' in order to make his point. The Westerner does not indicate that he is receptive, by returning Sipho's compliments, so both of them reach a conversational 'deadlock'.

Another example of the way cultural differences may affect the success of a personal conversation follows. African custom dictates that you must always say what is pleasing to your 'superior'. If, in a work situation, an African person is given an instruction and is asked: 'Do you understand?', the answer will always be 'yes', even if he or she does not understand. It would be considered impolite to be honest and say 'no'. This cultural rule frequently creates confusion and frustration between African and Western people.

Conversational greetings vary a great deal between cultures. African people would regard the indifference and the expedient politeness of the following scenario as very strange and rude. A Western person walks down a passage and ignores everyone because he is making a bee-line for Mr Smith. He cannot find Mr Smith, comes back, and greets the African person he had ignored a few minutes ago, and asks him where Mr Smith might be. Some Westerners, however, may also find such expedient politeness rather false.

There are different types of greeting mannerisms. In Zulu greeting behaviour, the senior person greets first. The junior person looks away until he or she is addressed. Such behaviour would be interpreted as rude by Westerners who might expect to be greeted first by those younger than themselves.[6]

Try now to reflect on the cultural 'rules' that apply to you. Think, for example, of the rules for *interrupting* people in your culture, or in your own family. Is it considered unacceptable to interrupt someone else while they are speaking? Do you apologize if you find yourself interrupting? Do men interrupt more often than women? Is it acceptable if older people interrupt the conversation of younger people, or vice versa?

What is regarded by some people as rude, and therefore as a failure in conversation, may be regarded as perfectly acceptable by others. Being sensitive to cultural issues is an important requirement if you want to be a successful conversationalist.

Prolonged silence is embarrassing in English conversations but quite normal in the conversations of other cultures. A point about silence in conversation is illustrated in the extract below:

Silence

In discussing rules of speaking, a good starting point would be the rules governing silence: when to speak and when not to speak, and how silence is interpreted.

The American tends to interpret silence negatively. Karl Reisman compares American and Scandinavian attitudes towards silence in a conversation:

> *Many Americans (and many English people) have a rule that in social conversations silences must be filled. A silence maintained too long is a sign of some kind of failure of rapport (unless it is defined as somehow seeking the solution to a problem...) In Denmark by contrast there is a tendency to treat silences as valuable signs – perhaps of the well being of those present, at least a kind of affirmation that people speak only when moved to do so, that their feelings are genuine ... Some Danes appear to 'nourish' a silence as one might appreciate a cosy fire.*

Discussing the relation of silence and privacy, Edward T. Hall points out that:

> *When the American wants to be alone he goes into a room and shuts the door ... For an American to refuse to talk to someone else present in the same room, to give them the 'silent treatment', is the ultimate form of rejection and a sure sign of great displeasure.*

In contrast, the Arab and the Englishman may achieve privacy through silence:

> *Their way to be alone is to stop talking. Like the English, an Arab who shuts himself off in this way is not indicating that anything is wrong or that he is withdrawing, only that he wants to be alone with his own thoughts or does not want to be intruded upon.*

Citing another instance of our negative evaluation of silence, Edmund Glenn says:

If you express an opinion and there is a little silence and then the subject is changed, you know you have said something with which the person you are talking to does not agree. In many other cultures, in contrast, silence is a sign of agreement. When the Russians, French, Portuguese, Spanish or Italians express an opinion and you do not reject it explicitly, they assume you have accepted it. Later, when they find you haven't they feel you are hypocritical.

This is true of Moroccans and Persians, too. But the Egyptian, like the American, interprets silence here as disagreement.

In the Orient there is a tradition of respectful silence before elders, and especially before teachers. An American teacher might well be disconcerted by the silence of Oriental students in an otherwise talkative class in the United States. Much the same is true of Latin American students. By this strategy of silence, the student does not show his ignorance by asking questions; he does not lose face by volunteering possibly wrong information, and he does not imply that the teacher's original explanations are unclear by asking for restatements. But he is not necessarily inattentive or uninterested.[7]

CONVERSATIONAL TURNS AND EXCHANGES IN ENGLISH

As we have said, most people are so familiar with the 'rules' and patterns of conversation that they are seldom *consciously* aware of them. However, conversational manoeuvres and turn-taking strategies definitely exist.

Conversations proceed along structured lines, with an opening, middle, and end. The 'rules' or 'conversational moves' that govern these interactions include the way conversations are started: 'I haven't seen you for ages – how are things going?' or 'What have you been doing lately?' Some opening strategies are mere pretexts to initiate a conversation: 'Do you have the time, please?' or 'Lovely evening, isn't it?'

For a conversation to be satisfying for the participants, everyone must have a chance to speak. When one person dominates or 'holds the floor', conversation ceases. Conversation, by its very nature, must involve exchange, like the hitting back and forth of a ball when playing tennis. Indeed, a conversation can be compared to a game with rules that all players must respect. Participants in this verbal game must be sensitive to *turn-taking*, and know when it is appropriate to speak, and when to stay silent and allow others to talk. Turn-taking is an essential characteristic of a successful conversation.

A general attitude of tolerance and co-operation should prevail in a conversation. If a speaker is not making himself or herself clear, the listeners should be patient, and perhaps help by prompting. Phrases such as: 'Let's get that straight – do you mean ...?' help the speaker to clarify the point. Similarly, a speaker who senses that the listeners do not understand what he or she is saying, might say: 'Are you with me?' or 'Let me give you an example ...'

The strategies speakers use to make others listen include: 'You'll never believe what happened to me yesterday...' or 'Guess what!' To change a topic, a speaker may say: 'Talking of schools, did you see in the paper that ...', or 'By the way ...'.

Listening is not a passive process. To indicate that they are interested in what is being said, good listeners may offer encouraging responses like: 'Yes...', 'Goodness...', 'You don't mean it!', and 'Honestly?' They make use of supportive expressions such as: 'I know exactly how you must have felt ...' to show the speaker that they empathize. Linguistic studies have shown that women offer much more conversational support than men, by making more frequent 'hmm hmm' noises and nodding their heads more than men, to convey understanding and interest.

Non-verbal or *paralinguistic* messages such as head nodding are an important part of conversation. If you watch people talking you will see how *body movements* such as leaning forwards; making hand and arm gestures; moving the head; making facial expressions; and grunting or 'tut-tutting' all show involvement in the conversation and communicate valuable messages. Phonological aspects of the *speech* itself, such as pitch, loudness, or speed can also enhance communication. Conversely, non-verbal messages can also contradict verbal messages and cause confusion.

There are different ways in which speakers and listeners can indicate either that they are ready to stop talking ('yield the floor'), or that they wish to be the next person to speak. The desire to speak next is some-times shown by an obvious intake of breath. Participants in a conversation also give clear signals when they feel a conversation has gone on long enough and must end: 'I'm so sorry, but I promised to meet someone at five, so I must be going …' or 'Well, it's been lovely talking to you again, but …' To simply stop and move away is rude and would be breaking the unwritten 'rules' of conversation. Frequently, a speaker may prepare the other parties for his or her departure in advance by glancing at a watch and saying things like: 'Gosh, it's getting late, I'll have to be going soon …'

Topics of conversation are also constrained by socio-cultural factors. Again, there are unwritten laws that make certain subjects acceptable but others taboo. (More will be said about taboos in Chapter 7.) If a group of people are relatively strange to one another, they will keep to 'safe' topics. This why a neutral subject such as the weather is so popular as an opening gambit among English speakers. Until the parties find out more about the others in the group, they are likely to exercise caution in their choice of topics. A group of young men meeting over a few beers after work might talk openly about their salaries and sex lives, but such candour in another group – perhaps made up of older people, and perhaps of mixed genders – may be frowned upon and regarded as a serious breach of 'correct' conversational conduct.

Activity 3 What makes a conversation successful

Draw a mind-map to summarize the factors that contribute to conversational success.

Activity 4 Conversational turns and exchanges

1 English conversation and analysis

Observe a real-life English conversation and analyse it in terms of what you have read in this chapter. What indications did the speakers use to indicate that they were ready to stop or start speaking? What fillers did they use? What other non-fluency features did you notice?

You could do this by writing down the names of the speakers and what they say. Follow this by an indication of the type of signal they give to show that they intend to stop speaking or that they wish to speak next, for example:

Speaker A:	*This is what I think we should do. Do you agree?*	A looks directly at B.
Speaker B:	*Well, er, I'm not sure. If you remember…*	B uses a filler (voiced pause).
	the last time …	Pauses
Speaker A:	*What do you mean?*	A leans forward and interrupts B.

Base your answer here on a real-life conversation.

2 Conversations in languages other than English

Are you familiar with languages other than English? We would like you to draw up your own list of 'rules' for turns and exchanges in the languages you have knowledge of. Are there differences between English and the other language(s)? For example, when a listener wants an opportunity to speak, does he or she wait to be invited to speak? Would it be acceptable to interrupt? Is silence considered rude, or is it acceptable? Try to give as much detail as you can.

Activity 5 Your description of a good conversationalist

1 Now we would like you to describe the characteristics of a 'good' English conversationalist. You would need to consider your ideal person as a speaker and as a listener. Please try to include as much detail as you can. Here are a few things you could think of:

- **Fluency**
  Does the conversationalist's conversation flow smoothly?

- **Sensitivity**
  Listeners need to speak. Is the conversationalist willing to allow them to do so?

- **Indicators (stopping)**

  What are the ways that indicate that the conversationalist is about to stop?

- **Indicators (listening)**

  What are the ways that indicate that the conversationalist is listening to the speaker?

2 If you speak more than one language, consider whether your 'good' conversationalist would have different habits for different languages and cultures.

THE FUNCTION OF CONVERSATION

We would like to relate the points we have made about conversation to the points made earlier in Chapter 3 about the *functions* of language. Much conversation has a *social* function, and certain language forms are used to establish or maintain *relationships* between people. (You may wish to glance back to Chapter 3 where we mention this *phatic* function of language.)

What is important in this kind of communication is that people respond to others by *listening to what they mean* and *interacting with them as they intended*, rather than merely responding detachedly to the words themselves. It would be a valuable exercise for you to analyse some examples of communication that you listen to or are a part of, with this in mind. The pointers below may help you to focus on this *phatic* or social function of language.

1 When someone sneezes, it is customary among English speakers for someone present to say 'Bless you!' How would you react if you said that, and the person who had sneezed replied, 'Who do you think you are – the Pope?' Would you be amused or offended? Either way, you might feel that the person in question had broken some unwritten 'rule' of behaviour for speaking English.

2   When someone hurts themselves in the company of another, whose primary language is an African language, the African language speaker would say 'Sorry!' in English (or in their primary language) even though they know they are not to blame for the injury. This is an expression of sympathy.

As an English speaker or a speaker of an African language or another language, have you ever had this experience? What would you consider the appropriate response to such an injury? Would it be rude for the injured person to say 'What are you apologizing for? It wasn't *your* fault'?

3   How do you feel about the ritual English greetings 'How are you?' and 'How do you do'? Do you think they have become meaningless? Or do you think they still serve their original purpose? If you speak to someone more than once a day, how many times can you ask how they are?

People who attend to customers in shops sometimes use the expression 'Have a nice day!' after completing a transaction. What do you think is an appropriate response? The person seeing to your needs has most probably been on their feet for several hours and will continue to be for some time before taking a long journey home. Do you think it is appropriate in this case to reply with the response 'You too!'?

IMPLICATURES

During the course of a conversation, the parties concerned often understand things that are *not* said. People pick up information that is not stated, but is *implied*. Pieces of unstated information are known as 'implicatures'. (The noun 'implicature' is derived from the verb 'imply'.) We all use implicatures unconsciously in everyday life.

Consider the following example of a conversational exchange between a man (A) and a woman (B):

A: *I'm starving.*
B: *I haven't been to the shops yet.*

On the surface, these two statements seem quite unconnected. What has going to the shops got to do with A's state of hunger?

When A says he's starving, it appears he expects B to take action by supplying him with food. This is an assumption probably based on their usual roles. B understands this implicature, but knows the cupboard is bare because she has not bought any food. By telling A she has not been to the shops, she is in effect stating that she has no food to offer. She assumes that A will understand this implicature, even though she does not state it explicitly.

Implicatures are another example of the unconscious way we observe conversational 'rules'. What these simple and apparently insignificant examples are intended to show is that we take a lot of implicit communication for granted in our conversations. We mean, and understand, much more than is actually said in the words that we utter.

Many jokes rely on implicatures for their humorous effect. The listener to the joke has to fill in the gap, or infer the implicature, in order to 'catch' the joke. Consider the following cartoon strip:

Pretoria News

What is the implicature in this joke?

By refusing to hand in his axe at the entrance of the restaurant for the reason that he has had steak there before, Hagar is implying that he will need his axe to cut the steak. So, the unstated piece of information, or implicature *is that the steaks at that restaurant are very tough.* This fact is implied much to the displeasure of the restaurant manager.

Activity 6 Implicatures

Explain the implicatures in the following exchanges:

1   A: *What's the time?*
       B: *The news is over.*

2   A: *Was that thunder I heard?*
       B: *I must close the windows.*
       A: *I'm sorry, I'm busy.*

3

HAGAR THE HORRIBLE   by Chris Browne

Pretoria News

(You will find suggested answers at the end of the book.)

SUMMARY

Here are the main points dealt with in this chapter:

- Spoken language has different characteristics from written language.
- Each form of language has its own purposes and merits.
- Attitudes towards speech and writing differ.
- Conversation is interactive and governed by certain 'rules'.
- Conversational 'rules' are influenced by cultural norms.
- Seemingly meaningless fillers have potent meanings and effects in successful conversation.
- Listening is an integral part of meaningful conversation.
- Implicatures commonly occur in conversations when the parties draw inferences about things that are not explicitly stated.

GLOSSARY

Fill in the correct meanings of the following:

phoneme
_____
_____

phonetics
_____
_____

articulatory phonetics
_____
_____

phonology
_____
_____

phonic
_____
_____

graphic
_____
_____

non-fluency features
_____
_____

fillers
_____
_____

false starts
_____
_____

paralinguistic features
_____
_____

emoticons
_____
_____

implicatures
_____
_____

ENDNOTES

1   HAYAKAWA, S. I. 1965. *Language in thought and action* (2ND edition) p. 10. London: George Allen and Unwin.

2   Ibid., p. 12.

3   Ibid., p. 14.

4   This discussion on written and spoken language is adapted from Crystal's discussion in *The Cambridge Encyclopedia of Language*, 1987, Chapter 31. Cambridge: Cambridge University Press.

5   DU PREEZ, H. 1997. *Meet the rainbow nation*, p. 22. Pretoria: Kagiso Tertiary.

6   Ibid., p. 87.

7   APPLEGATE, R. P. 1975. 'The language teacher and the rules of speaking' in the *TESOL Quarterly*. Vol. 9, No. 3, September, pp. 272–73.

7 **Does language have power?**

CHAPTER OUTLINE

So far we have paid quite a lot of attention to attitudes towards language and language use. This chapter deals with the power that language has to shape perceptions, as well as to shock, hurt and offend.

LEARNING OUTCOMES

By the end of this chapter you should have the following knowledge, skills, values, and attitudes:

Knowledge

You should understand
- why there is a widespread belief in the special powers of language
- how language can shape perceptions
- why language can persuade, shock, hurt, and offend
- the power and importance of language taboos
- what is meant by political correctness
- the way language is used to represent ethnicity, and
- the importance of place names, and the different attitudes towards name change.

Skills

You should be able
- to describe your own language taboos
- to recognize and understand euphemisms, and
- to recognize opinions and points of view underlying discussion.

Values and attitudes

You should develop
- respect and tolerance for the language taboos of others
- sensitivity to the use of racial or sexist terms, and
- respect and tolerance for various attitudes towards changes of place names.

INTRODUCTION

In every culture there is a belief that language has special powers. In Chapter 3, we discussed one of the functions of language: 'the control of reality' when language is used to make an occasion 'real', or when the use of certain language invests an occasion with special significance. For example, before a witness gives evidence in court, he or she has to take a verbal oath, and swear on the Bible 'to tell the truth, the whole truth and nothing but the truth'. Such customs and procedures imply respect for the power of language, which can bind people in important ways. Some prayers as well as praise songs and anthems have a specific form and are always repeated in exactly the same way. There are also certain forms of worship that follow a particular pattern of statement and response.

Undoubtedly, language has power. We have only to call to mind the way a crowd can be emotionally swayed, inflamed or urged to action by a skilled orator to realize that language can indeed create, reinforce, or change perceptions and influence behaviour.

Perhaps less dramatic, more subtle, but no less powerful (because of the widespread influence of the mass media), is the effect that the language used in advertising can have on consumers. Opinions held by the public can be manipulated by clever use of emotive language. Manufacturers and advertisers in many parts of the world spend enormous amounts of money every year on advertising goods and products. This suggests that the advertisers have reason to believe in the power of advertising to influence people's buying habits.

Why do government or church authorities sometimes ban or censor the writings of certain authors? Would you agree that it is because they believe that these writings will influence the people who read them, either politically or morally, and cause public dissent? The laws that limit freedom of the press, and enforce censorship in some countries, certainly imply this belief.

The article below that appeared in the *Pretoria News* of 8 October 1999, deals with legislation, proposed at that time, in South Africa. We have included it here as an indication that South African authorities have recognized the power of language. However, the article also points out that censoring certain forms of language may take away people's rights to freedom of expression.

What do *you* think? Do people need to be protected against the power of language? Or should their freedom of expression be protected? Does society need to maintain a balance?

New racism Bill 'will affect media freedom'

CAPE TOWN, New equality legislation due to be tabled in Parliament within weeks will clamp down on racism in the media, including print, radio and television, art works and the Internet.

But human rights campaigners fear the Promotion of Equality and Prevention of Unfair Discrimination Bill casts its net so wide it may also infringe on the constitutionally-enshrined right to freedom of expression.

The Bill prohibits the publication of any matter deemed discriminatory, and gives the Minister of Justice the power to issue guidelines for the media to ensure compliance.

It also bans the use of 'hurtful and abusive' words such as 'kaffir', 'bobbejaan', 'meid', 'coolie', 'hotnot' and 'boer'.

The Bill, which has been approved by the cabinet, has to be passed into law by March next year.

The Freedom of Expression Institute (FXI) said it was concerned by the implications for freedom of expression and has referred the Bill to its legal advisers.

FXI executive director, Laura Pollecutt, said the Bill, if passed in its present form, could have a 'devastating' effect on media freedom.

'It gives carte blanche to introduce legislation which could inhibit the freedom of the media,' she said.

'We will study the Bill and make a substantive input in the committee stage.'

The Bill defines media as 'any speech or any form of communication which seeks to convey a message or expression of ideas, opinion or beliefs', including works of art, advertisements, newspapers and magazines, radio and television and the Internet.

It prohibits unfair discrimination in the media 'in any manner', including the publication of 'propaganda, ideas or theories based on unfair racial stereotypes' or the dissemination of information which promotes inequality or incites prejudice against people on the basis of race, ethnicity, gender or religion.

This means the media could be barred from reporting on racist or sexist speeches.

It also prohibits the media from 'violating the privacy' of any person by publishing information, without the permission of the person concerned, which could impair that person's dignity or which falls under any of the grounds of unfair discrimination listed in the Bill.

This means journalists would not be able to include biographical details about a person, such as that he or she is married, has children, or is single, without the subject's permission.

It could also preclude the use of phrases such as 'elderly', 'effeminate', 'youthful', 'wheelchair-bound' or 'sickly' without permission.

Pretoria News, 8 October, 1999

The legislation discussed in the article on the new racism Bill exemplifies the movement towards 'political correctness' that has become a general feature of the modern world. Political correctness aims at using language with greater sensitivity, and eliminating discriminatory language previously used against minorities or disadvantaged people. On one hand this aims at representing certain individuals and groups in a more positive way, and recognizes everyone's need to be accorded respect. Underlying this awareness is the realization that language influences perceptions, and the hope that the use of respectful terms will increase sensitivity and respect among people. For example, instead of calling elderly people 'old', you would call them 'senior citizens', a more polite and respectful form of address.

On the other hand, however, political correctness has been taken too far in many cases and has become the subject of jokes. For example, it is unconstitutional to call someone 'crippled', but you can say they are 'mobility-impaired'. It is politically incorrect to describe someone as 'short', so the phrase 'vertically challenged' has come into use. Some feel that certain politically correct expressions are nothing short of absurd.

With regard to racial issues, however, political correctness is a significant characteristic of the 'new' South Africa, and for good reason. Given our divided history, and the racially embedded thinking enshrined in the legislation of the previous government, it is not surprising that notions of 'race' persist, sometimes to the point of obsession. 'Race' continues to be a highly sensitive issue in the post-apartheid period. Attempts to break down negative racial attitudes are reflected in the new laws, which outlaw racist terminology.

Activity 1 Abusive terms

The above article refers to abusive terms such as 'meid' and 'boer'. How and why are these terms offensive? Have they always been so, or have their original connotations changed? Are there some contexts in which these words can still legitimately be used?

(Compare your ideas with those suggested at the end of the book.)

The article refers to 'unfair racial stereotyping'. What does this phrase mean?

The *Oxford Advanced Learner's Dictionary* defines 'stereotype' as 'a fixed idea or image that many people have of a particular type of person or thing, but which is often not true in reality'. Many terms denoting ethnicity are stereotypical. A person perceived in terms of a particular and often racial characteristic, is stereotyped. For example, when a 'Coloured' person is referred to by the racial term 'kroeskop', such an individual is perceived in terms of one single physical characteristic (in this case, hair). This single characteristic is regarded as an 'ethnic

marker'. The label focuses on only one particular feature. To label someone in this way, is to force them into a category and generalize about
them on the basis of one superficial attribute. This diminishes them as
human beings (or dehumanizes them). The regular use of such negative
labelling reinforces and spreads negative attitudes and prejudice. This is
why the Bill discussed in the above article outlaws the use of such terms.

The article leads us into a discussion of 'verbal taboos'. Such taboos
imply a recognition of the power of language.

VERBAL TABOOS

What do we understand by the word 'taboo'? What is the origin of this
word? What is the difference between a *taboo* and a *verbal taboo*?

The word 'taboo' comes from Tongan, and means 'holy' or 'untouch-
able'. Taboos are topics that society wants to avoid. Taboo behaviour
refers to behaviour that is forbidden in a certain society or cultural
group. *Verbal taboos* refer to terms that are considered unacceptable and
may not be used in speech. *The Oxford Advanced Learner's Dictionary*
defines 'taboo' thus:

> **taboo**/ *noun* **1** a cultural or religious custom that does not allow
> people to do, use, or talk about a particular thing as people find
> it offensive or embarrassing: *an incest taboo* ◊ *a taboo on working
> on Sunday* ◊ *to break/violate a taboo* ◊ *Death is one of the great taboos
> in our culture.* **2** a general agreement not to do sth or talk about
> sth: *The subject is still a taboo in this family.*
> **taboo** *adj.*: *in the days when sex was a **taboo subject**.*
> **taboo words** *noun* [pl.] words that many people consider
> offensive or shocking, for example because they refer to sex, the
> body, or people's race.

Taboos are closely linked to culture and are formed by the people and
culture to which they belong. This means that what is taboo in one society may be perfectly acceptable in another. For example, in Muslim
communities it is not permissible to eat or even talk about pigs, whereas

the eating of pork or discussing pigs is regarded as absolutely normal in many other cultures.

Taboos may change with the passing of time. For example, during the days of our parents and grandparents, open discussion of sex was taboo, but today sex is discussed much more openly. It is interesting to reflect that the necessity to speak openly about sex in order to help slow down the spread of HIV/Aids, and to prevent death from Aids, has certainly helped to speed up the process of removing the taboo. In the interests of controlling further HIV infection, schoolchildren are given detailed information regarding sexual behaviour in explicit terms. At the time of writing, a radio campaign is in operation, which uses well-known celebrities to urge listeners to 'love your children enough to talk about sex'. This concept would have been unthinkable thirty years ago. This is a case where the needs of health have overridden socio-cultural and linguistic taboos, resulting in changed behaviour and a changed society. The powerful and daunting issue of HIV/Aids has given rise to other language changes, as we will be discussing later.

It is not difficult to illustrate the existence and power of verbal taboos: the fact that it would be difficult or impossible to print certain examples in this book is evidence enough. Which taboo are *you* most aware of in social situations? Do you think people are more concerned about avoiding certain *topics* or about avoiding specific *words* and *expressions*? Do you think there are different 'rules' for different groups of people and for different social situations? Can you think of examples where there are different 'rules' for different age groups? Would you agree that the 'rules' of acceptability have changed over the years?

Since we are distinguishing between taboo *subjects* (topics) and taboo *words*, we should stop to think about the feelings associated with some words. Most words have a *denotative* meaning, which we may think of as the 'dictionary definition' of that word. For example, the word 'leg' in English can be used to *refer* to something tangible in the real world, namely, the limb of a human being or animal that is used for standing, walking, and running. This denotative meaning of a word (also called its 'referential meaning' from the word *refer*) is considered *neutral* or without any associated feelings.

However, some words have more than just their denotations or denotative meanings. If a word is considered unacceptable, it is partly because people have been taught to feel certain *emotions* when they hear this word spoken. Feelings of fear may be associated with the mention of death, for example, and feelings of shame or embarrassment may be associated with references to sex or to other bodily functions. The feelings that may accompany a word in this way are referred to as the *connotations* of that word. The example we have just used, the word 'leg', has hardly any connotations these days, but for the Victorians a leg was a highly sexual and unmentionable part of a woman's anatomy that had to be kept covered at all times.

The names of other parts of the body may call up a variety of different emotions. Is this why some parents use 'pet names' or 'family names' to refer to their children's 'private parts'? (Our use of the term 'private parts' is a substitute for 'genitals', and a way of avoiding the use of the word 'genitals'.)

We have listed and discussed below some topics that some people may feel uncomfortable talking about, and describe some of the ways in which such topics are usually referred to.

Sex

Most people belong to several different social groups, which may have different 'rules' for language use and behaviour. People seem to be able to move from one group to another with relative ease. For example, one group to which most people belong is the family, which has certain values and traditions that are shared and respected. A person from a particular family could find himself or herself in another group when he or she goes to work, for example, and could move into yet other groups in social situations. When people watch films and television, they temporarily join a much larger group: an enormous audience made up of people all over the country or even the Western world.

What does this have to do with the topic of verbal taboos about sex and related issues? You are likely to find that the topic of sex is treated very differently in different groups and situations. For example, many people may find that they are uncomfortable talking about sexual matters either to their parents, or in front of them. In this case, the *topic* itself would be avoided. The same people might find it easier to talk freely about sex and related issues with their friends and peers, thus removing the taboo on the topic itself. However, some people would still experience a certain sense of restraint or embarrassment, and would use alternative words that would enable them to discuss sex indirectly (without referring explicitly to parts of the body or to specific sexual acts).

What about biology lessons at school? The term 'sexual reproduction' would obviously not be taboo, but the language used would be of a technical or scientific nature. Parts of the body that form the reproductive system would be mentioned in a neutral, unemotional way in this context, using the denotative or referential meaning of the appropriate words. This illustrates the importance of *context* in deciding whether or not it is appropriate to discuss certain topics and in what terms they are discussed.

There are also situations in which people freely use certain taboo words associated with sex (such as the so-called f-word in English) and yet do not use them to discuss the topic of sex at all. Sometimes the 'f-word' and other so-called four-letter words are used to express anger, frustration, or contempt for something or someone. This practice has become quite common in certain movies. Such words have a very strong connotative value, and are considered taboo in many social groups and circumstances. Where is the taboo in this case? Is it the word or the topic? Our avoidance of the printing of these words in full is itself expressive of the taboo.

Since HIV/Aids has become a matter for urgent discussion worldwide, the fear of death from Aids has superseded the fear or taboo of using explicit sexual words and terms, in general conversation. Hence the recent removal of the taboo on such words and phrases as 'condom' and 'unprotected sex'.

Death

Do you find that many people are uncomfortable talking about the *topic* of death, or are there certain *words* associated with death that they often try to avoid? Some people, even when they have to mention someone's death when relating the event or when giving information, still prefer to avoid the word *die* and any of its forms. Common alternative phrases are 'passing away' or 'passing on'. These would suggest that the people who use them believe or would prefer not to believe that death is final, or believe that death does not exist at all.

The name of God

Some religious groups avoid any mention of the name of God, whereas others have strict rules about only mentioning the name of God in special circumstances. However, it sometimes happens that the name of God is used freely in English to express something quite different, such as surprise, extreme emotion (either positive or negative), horror, or shock. This practice is not considered acceptable by those who regard this kind of talk as 'blasphemous'. The name of God 'taken in vain' occurs quite frequently, for example, in certain movies.

Many people feel extremely uncomfortable and even offended when the name of God is used in this way. What has created the taboo in this case? Is it the fact that the *word* is not being associated with its original *meaning*? Is it the fact that the word is not being used with the *awe* and *respect* with which it was originally used, and is still used by many?

References to race

Some words used by members of one racial group to refer to people of another race group can carry an enormous weight of emotional meaning or connotation. Examples of such words are familiar to members of South African society, and it is not surprising that, in the context of South African history, these words are highly controversial and arouse strong reactions. As we saw in the article about the new equality legislation, words like 'kaffir', 'coolie' and 'hotnot' are now banned. These words are all examples of *ethnic terminology*. Inevitably, in South Africa, ethnicity evokes the concept of skin colour.

People with a strong sense of ethnic identity show this through their use of language, which reflects the way they perceive themselves and others. Some see their own behaviour and culture as the 'norm', and the behaviour and culture of others as not only different, but 'abnormal'. This creates an opposition between 'us' and 'them'.

The 'we' group (the 'inside' group) make use of *marked terminology*[1] to describe the 'others', or the outside group. 'Marked terminology' means that the ethnicity of the 'other' is specifically stated. When members of the 'inside group' refer to themselves, however, they use 'unmarked' terminology, which means that their own ethnic identity is not mentioned. The 'we' group's identity is 'invisible' because it is felt to be 'normal'.

As an illustration of the use of marked and unmarked ethnicity, consider the following example from the press on the topic of crime in the area of Witpoortjie:

On blockwatch patrol, the language too, is different.

Recalling their experiences, white patrollers say: "A black jumped over that wall."

Black patrollers say: "A guy jumped over that wall."

They both mean black men, but the whites make a point about the race. It's not said to prove a point about the profile of the suburban criminal, it's said to make the criminal sound more desperate, and the crime more likely to have caused bloodshed and trauma had the block-watch not saved the day.

Sunday Times, 30 September, 2001

When 'marked' terminology denoting a particular ethnic group is used in connection with undesirable behaviour, the reader's or listener's perceptions are influenced. This is how topics such as crime become 'over-ethnicized'.

It would be a useful exercise if you were to analyse your own emotions on hearing or reading offensive racial terms. Use the (shortened) excerpt from the *Sunday Times* newspaper below as an example. Do you feel rage, hurt, embarrassment, shame, or amusement? The feeling you experience would be a good indication of your own position in relation to racial issues, conflict, or discrimination.

Tape of shame

THIS is an edited transcript, translated from the original Afrikaans, of the conversation between former Griqualand West rugby captain André Bester and former South African Springbok coach André Markgraaff, recorded on 22 October, 1996.

B: *Look, the guys who are attacking you are the English press. They attack you. That George.*
(Silence)
B: *The rest is just about cricket.*
M: I do not care what the f*** they are saying.

B: *Listen, but the guys who are attacking you are from the English press, man.*

M: No mate. I am a f****** rugby guy. I am not a politician ... I told him ... I cannot play f****** political games ... I feel f***-all for politics.

B: *Why are you saying that?*

M: No, ag Jesus, everything is politics, man. The whole f****** Pienaar and all. I do not want to get involved in politics.

B: *How is the Pienaar-thing political?*

M: Of course it is f****** politics. The whole f****** country is behind him ... in terms of the press.

B: *Yes.*

M: Top Sport is the media. TV is the ... is the government. Top Sport is the government. It is a kaffir station, it's the kaffirs ... Edward Griffiths works for Top Sport. David van der Sandt, the whole lot, everything. The government, the whole f****** lot, it's the government. That guy, (he) can be walking on f****** crutches, but they will still f****** want him.

B: *Oh, you think it's the government ...Griffiths behind the whole thing.*

M: Of course, yes.

B: *Listen, André, tell me.*

M: Now I hear Mluleki George wants to f****** resign on Friday. It's the kaffirs, man, it is the f****** NSC, it's the f****** kaffirs.
B: Now listen here, tell me quickly, mmm. If you had known about this whole debacle, would you not rather have chosen Pienaar?

M: Not a f***, not a f***.

B: *He did not play shit against Northern Transvaal, he did not play badly.*

M: Yes, but he played shit for 14 months. They are the best team in the country, look how they are f****** playing. They failed to make it to the Currie Cup final with 14 World Cup players, that was last year.

Sunday Times, 23 February, 1997

The article is very thought-provoking, because the words 'kaffir' and 'shit', which most people would consider taboo, were printed in full. The word 'Jesus' is also used, breaking a religious taboo. Christians would regard this as blasphemy. How can we explain the editor's policy here, especially his use of 'kaffir'?

The explanation lies in the *date* of the report. You will see that it was printed in 1997. The legislation discussed in the report that we reproduced earlier in this chapter ('New racism Bill will affect media freedom') came into force in 1999, two years later. The term 'kaffir' was offensive in 1997, but it was not actually illegal. This is a good example of the way language reflects changing attitudes in society. You may remember that in the news report '*Gatvol* slips into Parliament's lexicon' (quoted in Chapter 4) it was stated that 'at one time racism was government policy'. Nowadays, the use of racist terms can get one into serious trouble with the law. For the very reasons referred to above, historical context has to be taken into account when considering whether or not a particular term was or is offensive.

However, to return to the Markgraaff incident, the editor seems to feel that the readers, who are strong enough to deal with the use of the racial slur 'kaffir' and a direct reference to excrement in the word 'shit', are too delicate to read the four-letter 'f-word' referring to the sex act. It is also interesting to notice that this word is not used to denote the sex act at all in this context, but is merely used as an insult to express anger and frustration (or illustrates the inability to express anger and frustration articulately). One can't help wondering how the same readers deal with movies in which the 'f-word' is used freely in this way. Do the readers really need to be 'protected' by the three asterisks used to represent the missing letters (***)? Should the editor have used the same device to avoid printing the words 'Jesus', 'kaffir' and 'shit' as well?

What do *you* think? Are all these words equally unacceptable or acceptable in your view? Do you have different feelings about the connotations and appropriateness of these words? When you watch films or television, do you think that the scenes and actions portrayed are more or less offensive than the language spoken (if they are offensive at all)? The letter to the editor, reproduced below, may help to start you thinking about your own responses to the topic. It appeared in the *Mail & Guardian* newspaper of 13 to 19 August, 1999.

Acceptable language?

THIS MORNING I was searching the Web for various newspapers from around the world, and I found the *M&G* of South Africa.

I proceeded to check the various news items and the article 'Blacks in full colour', by Ngaire Blankenberg. I began to read and was stunned to find a certain word: 'The style of the films is pure funk, raw machismo with a *fuck you* attitude that recalls the real man heroes, like John Travolta, of the films of yesterday.'

I am wondering whether this is considered acceptable language in South Africa. And I will tell you that this word will never be found in any US newspaper.

Is this word part of the common language? Does it take on a different, lesser meaning in South Africa? I'm sure you are familiar with its meaning in the US, and perhaps you can understand why I question your use of the word.

Matt Arens, Springfield, Missouri, US
Mail & Guardian, 13–19 August, 1999

(The writer of this letter has responded to the use of this word in print, yet the same word is often spoken in American movies. Is it more acceptable to *hear* the 'f-word' (in films) than to *read* it in print?)

EUPHEMISMS AND CIRCUMLOCUTIONS

We have briefly mentioned how people deal with taboo subjects in such a way as to avoid having to use taboo words, such as using 'passing away' instead of 'death'. Most cultures have developed *euphemisms* and *circumlocutions*, expressions or words that refer to the taboo topic without using the words that express that topic directly.

- A *euphemism* is an indirect or mild way of referring to an unpleasant or unacceptable topic. The word comes from the Greek *eu*, meaning 'good', and *pheme* meaning 'speech' or 'saying'. Put together, euphemism means to 'speak with good words or in a pleasant manner'.

Euphemizing refers to the substitution of an explicit, offensive term with an inoffensive or pleasant one.

- A *circumlocution* is a way of saying something in many words, or in a roundabout manner so as to avoid having to refer directly or explicitly to the topic. Informally, we can also refer to this as 'beating around the bush', which means that excessive verbiage is used to save us having to name something shocking or embarrassing. An example we gave of politically correct language: 'mobility-impaired', instead of 'cripple' would fall into this category.

Euphemisms and circumlocutions are deliberately vague and indirect. For example, instead of saying outright that someone is a 'liar', you could use the euphemism: they are 'economical with the truth'. This is also a circumlocution, or a roundabout expression, using several words instead of just one to refer to the same thing. The crime of fraud has sometimes been referred to as 'creative accounting'.

A more sinister example related to the subject of warfare is the word *genocide*, where one group is intent on the mass killing of another national or racial group. In more than one conflict situation genocide has been called 'ethnic cleansing' or 'the final solution'. Both *cleansing* and *solution* have positive connotations, making them sound as though they are describing something pleasant and acceptable, but the horrific reality of the actual *killing* is deliberately overlooked and remains unspecified. The deliberate vagueness is intended to disguise the negative impact of killing, and the violence involved. Scientific vocabulary can also disguise the unpleasant or morbid connotations of ordinary expressions by giving them an unemotional and clinical tone. For example, the emotive word *abortion* is often referred to as TOP (termination of pregnancy).

Activity 2 Taboos and euphemisms

In the table below, we have listed some taboo topics in the middle column, together with the *euphemisms* and *circumlocutions* used to express these topics in the right-hand column. Add to this table if you can by giving your own examples. You may also use examples from languages other than English.

Language	Topic	Euphemism or circumlocution
English	death or dying (noun); to die (verb)	to go home to pass away to depart this life
English	to excrete	to visit the bathroom to relieve oneself to answer the call of nature
English	to kill	to eliminate to rub out to take out
English	to have sex	to go to bed with someone to sleep with someone to make love
English	a prostitute	an escort a lady of easy virtue a sex worker
English	to be drunk	to be happy/merry to be under the influence to be under the weather

RACIAL EUPHEMISMS

In South Africa in the last few years, you may have noticed how the writers of news reports have tended to refrain from using *marked terminology* to indicate race. At one time, references to race were always included. This is another sign of the new political correctness that has filtered into the media. Sometimes reference to race is so pointedly avoided that it compromises the clarity of the report. Journalists will sometimes make use of euphemisms or find another indirect way of conveying the ethnicity of the people they are writing about.

Activity 3 Job advertisement

Spot the euphemism in the following advertisement for employment:

EXECUTIVE SECRETARY
(AA ONLY)

- Presentable, competent secretary to work closely with Directors
- Computer literate with MS OFFICE, applications/MS Word skills essential
- Fully bilingual
- Needs to be able to work under pressure
- Typing speed at least 40 wpm
  Remuneration: R5 000 per month plus benefits.
  Interested applicants can apply to: ...

(Compare your answer with the one suggested at the end of the book.)

As we have said before, language is not static: it changes as society changes and new linguistic needs arise. New attitudes generate new terms. New euphemisms, reflecting new taboo subjects, come into being. The newspaper report below discusses one such example.

Stigma of Aids abates as deaths spiral

IN THE TOWNSHIPS of Cape Town it is called "iLotto" and "Omo Micro".

"iLotto" refers to the fact that to have sex is to gamble these days with Aids spreading. "Omo Micro" describes how the faces of some people with Aids becomes pale when they are close to death.

These words are just two of many codenames for HIV/Aids, and are used in the townships of Cape Town to avoid using the real name of the disease, because there is such a heavy stigma attached to it.

The stigma stems from the fact that HIV/Aids is seen as a result of promiscuity which is condemned by communities, according to researchers at the University of Cape Town and the University of the Western Cape.

Said Tania Vergnani, director of HIV/Aids programmes at the University of the Western Cape: "If HIV was transmitted in the same way as flu, there would be no stigma attached to it. This stigma is very real and alive. It is abating bit by bit, but not nearly fast enough, and lots of people are dying lonely and isolated. At university I can't get a single student to come out and say they are HIV positive – I think they are all scared."

"A lot of our students come from rural areas. They're terrified the news will get back to their communities, and their families will be ostracised."

Euphemisms for HIV/Aids

Among the euphemisms for HIV/Aids are:

- "iAce", like "iLotto", is a reference to sex being a gamble with the disease.
- *Tshivi* means HIV.
- "This thing" is often cited by family and friends as a reason for some-one's death, as it helps them avoid saying the word Aids directly.
- "This thing outside", or "she got the Lotto outside", is used by family members to inform others the disease was not contracted in their own homes.

Different codewords are used in different parts of South Africa. Mandla Majola, spokesman for the treatment Action Campaign lobby group, said the words are a form of 'superstition'. "People use the words because they don't want to say HIV/Aids," he said. "There is the fear people could be bewitched, or infected, just by saying the name."

Own Correspondent
Pretoria News, November 22, 2001

PROPER NAMES

Personal names have a particular kind of power. In some cultures, people do not like to hear or say their own names. This is because they feel that 'the whole of their being' resides in their name. If other people know and use their name, these people will have power over them, possibly power to do them harm.

PLACE NAMES

The names of countries, towns, and cities often remind people of important periods in their history. These periods may obviously be viewed by various members of the community as either good or bad times, and the names associated with those periods will also be regarded as favourable or unfavourable.

In recent South African history, this issue has received a lot of attention. As in many other parts of the world, local place names have been changed from time to time to express new social, historical, and political perceptions. Linked to the momentous political changes of 1994, names that reflected the colonial or apartheid past of our country have come under the spotlight. Many South Africans feel that keeping the names of old apartheid leaders such as H. F. Verwoerd is an affront to black people.

Activity 4 Place names

Below you will find a table with place names, some old, some new. Fill in the names in the spaces we have left blank, and add any more examples that you can think of.

Old	New
Hendrik Verwoerd Dam	Gariep Dam
	Johannesburg International Airport
Rhodesia	
	Namibia
Lourenço Marques	
John Vorster Square	
Pietersburg	
	Thaba Tshwane

ATTITUDES TOWARDS NAME CHANGES

As is natural, the changing of names arouses different reactions. Read the following newspaper texts (letters to the editor) in which some of these reactions are expressed.

Text 1

I REFER TO the report regarding the proposed renaming of Pretoria to Mandela City, to be spearheaded by the New Nationalist Party, according to their representative, one Max van der Walt.

A few years ago, the Nationalist Party turned their backs on Dr Hendrik Verwoerd and, against the wishes of the residents and rate-payers, changed the name Verwoerdburg into the meaningless Centurion to please and pacify the so-called business community.

If they think to get away so easily as in the case of Verwoerdburg, they are in for a surprise.

The electorate has already dealt with them for the way they have handed power over to the African National Congress/South African Communist Party alliance, and any further treacherous conduct will not be tolerated by the residents of Pretoria.

Jan Kriel, Pretoria
Mail & Guardian, 9–15 July, 1999

Text 2

THE BIGGER CHALLENGE facing South Africa and its cities is to break away from the colonial past.

This is in the light of the fact that there are symbols and names which still remind us and reflect days of suppression and oppression. Days when people were arrested for trivial offences.

The name "Pretoria" is derived from one coloniser and military leader of the Great Trek of the Afrikaner people. General Andries Wilhelmus Jacobus Pretorius, who was responsible for the destruction of Dingaan and many African kings and queens.

The name therefore honours a person who to many of us as Africans was responsible for the misery and pain that was inflicted on African people. The name Pretoria is also exclusive since it is not reflective and representative of the African majority.

If we are to have a new image as a city, people and a country we must move in line with the changes unfolding in the entire country where all of us will be part of and draw pride from any symbol and name that is used in our beloved country.

It goes without saying that Tshwane is the only name that has a history that is not repressive and that does not carry the stigma of Apartheid or any evil against humanity.

This also means that even the name of the country should change to truly reflect that we are breaking with the colonial past.

Azania remains the only legitimate name as a replacement of the colonial name South Africa, which denotes nothing but is a description of the location of the country on the continent and is a name that was imposed on the African majority.

Raymond Mashilo Kgagudi and Jacob Wistebaar, Pretoria
Pretoria News, 2 August, 1999

Text 3

WHY IS IT that organisations such as the Pan Africanist Congress and Azanian People's Organisation insist on referring to South Africa as 'Azania'? These organisations are supposedly in the forefront of the movement away from Eurocentrism, purporting to espouse Afrocentrism, and yet their aim is to give this country a Greek name. Why? What on earth for?

What is more, it is a name associated with a part of Greece notori-ous for the oppression of one group over all others, an early form of apartheid, in fact. As if this were not enough, it is also a name which came to be used to refer to parts of the Middle East and Northern Africa when they became sources of slaves.

It would thus seem to be no accident that these regions were at appropriate times dubbed 'Anzania'.

Terence Beard, Grahamstown
Mail & Guardian, 16–22 July, 1999

Text 4

ATHENS IS STILL Athens after more than 2000 years of changing ownership sporadically. So is Rome. And Jerusalem. Trier in Germany is simply
a Germanised form of Augusta Treverorum, the name given to it by the
Roman conquerors. No hard feelings.

The city of Pretoria would never have been, had it not been for one
Marthinus Wessel Pretorius, like it or not. The very reason Potgietersrus
came into existence was that Andries Hendrik Potgieter died there. How
does the government want to change that? Demolish the town, rebuild it
in African style (which one?) Pretend that an African king had died there,
and rename it?

The entire business becomes patently absurd, ridiculous and tragi-
comical. And costly, especially in provinces where people are dying of
hunger and Aids, where they have no water or electricity, where matric
results are non-existent and schools nearly so. Has a name change ever
made one iota of difference to the quality of life of the inhabitants?

Let Pretoria be Pretoria, and Letsitele remain Letsitele. It is cheaper
and wiser. Malaria, TB, Aids and survival are much more important issues.

Johan Viljoen, Queenswood
Pretoria News, 9 August, 1999

Activity 5 Place names: attitudes

Complete the table below, indicating whether the person/s concerned in each
case has/have a *positive* or *negative* attitude towards the *name changes* that
have been suggested in each case.

Name of person concerned	Positive or negative attitude towards the name change
1 Jan Kriel	
2 Raymond Mashilo Kgagudi and Jacob Wistebaar	
3 Terence Beard	
4 Johan Viljoen	

(You will find suggested answers at the end of this book.)

SUMMARY

Here is a summary of the main points discussed in this chapter:

- Language is seen as a very significant aspect of human life, one with special, even mystical, powers that control reality.
- Language taboos exist where topics and certain words are culturally and emotionally sensitive.
- Political correctness reflects ways in which people avoid explicit reference to unpleasant or sensitive topics.
- Language has the power to influence people's perceptions and behaviour.
- This power is used and acknowledged in legislation and censorship, and in the field of advertising, among others.
- Euphemisms and circumlocutions are ways of making unpleasant or sensitive words sound better.
- Race and ethnicity are highly sensitive concepts, and language trends illustrate this.
- Place names are highly political and can arouse strong emotions. For this reason, they are sometimes changed when governments change.

We would like to remind you of our earlier statements about the equality of languages, and about the importance of using *systematic analysis* of language facts to further the aims of tolerance and respect.

GLOSSARY

Here is a list of some important terms used in this chapter. Fill in the missing definitions and add other terms and definitions if you wish.

political correctness   _____

_____

racial stereotype   _____

_____

ethnicity   _____

_____

taboo   _____

_____

euphemism   _____

_____

circumlocution   _____

_____

ENDNOTES

1   THOMAS, LINDA AND WAREING, SHAN. 1999. *Language, society and power*, p. 87. London: Routledge.

8 Can grammar change meaning?

CHAPTER OUTLINE

In this chapter we are going to look at individual *words*: how they convey meaning, how they are made up, and how they combine to form meaningful *sentences*. The arrangement of words and the way they function together in sentences form the *grammar* of a language.

LEARNING OUTCOMES

By the end of this chapter you should have the following knowledge, skills, values, and attitudes:

Knowledge

You should understand

- the relationship between words and meaning
- the difference between denotation and connotation
- the meaning of emotive language
- the meaning of the term *morpheme*
- how words are divided into morphemes
- the difference between content words and structure words
- how grammatical function determines word class and meaning
- the different word-formation processes, and
- the meaning of grammar.

Skills

You should be able

- to understand and be sensitive towards the connotations of different words and emotive language
- to recognize how cultural differences affect meaning

- to analyse words into their constituent morphemes, and to understand how morphemes affect meaning
- to recognize different word-formation processes, and
- to recognize the grammatical functions of words in sentences.

Values and attitudes

You should develop

- an appreciation of the patterns and organization found in the structure of sentences
- recognition of the fact that language does not fit neatly into simple categories, and
- respect for the diversity of language usage in different cultural contexts.

INTRODUCTION

Words are the building blocks of language. When learning a language we gradually learn the meanings of different words, and build up a 'mental dictionary' in our memories. This mental dictionary is a store of words that represent concrete objects and abstract concepts. This important relationship – between words and their meanings – seems to be such an obvious one it hardly needs comment.

However, the study of the relationship between words and meaning – known as *semantics* – is not simple. *Semantics* is a complex field of study that explores the extensive relationship between words, phrases, and systems – and the world.

SOME SEMANTIC ISSUES

A fundamental semantic concept that we all probably take for granted is that the connection between the word and the thing it stands for is completely *arbitrary*. This means that the pairing of a particular sound (or written sign) with a meaning is usually a matter of complete chance, and has not come about for any necessarily logical reason.

For example, in English, a dog could just as well be called 'cat', and a cat could just as easily have been named 'mouse' or 'zeg'. We become so used to the meaning of words it is quite unsettling to question the process and realize that a beloved pet could equally have been called 'monster', or that ice-cream could have been named 'spinach' or something that seems equally incongruous. However, the only reason these words would strike you as 'incongruous' is because you have become used to associating the words 'monster' and 'spinach' with totally different concepts in your mind.

DENOTATION AND CONNOTATION

Another reason you would find it odd to use the word 'monster' to name a pet – apart from the fact that you would just not be used to making this semantic connection – is that words have *connotative* as well as *denotative* meanings.

As we mentioned in Chapter 7 (pages 139–140), the *denotation* of a word is its literal, 'dictionary meaning', whereas the *connotations* of a word are its emotional associations. The word 'pet' has positive connotations – we associate pets with companionship and affection – while the word 'monster' has negative connotations. From childhood we probably learned to associate monsters with ugliness and danger, and may still have feelings of fear and aversion towards them! For these associative reasons, it would be difficult for us to suddenly switch to calling a pet a 'monster'.

The denotative meanings of words are *objective,* while the connotations of words are *subjective.* On one hand most people would agree on the denotative meaning of a particular word, because it is *neutral,* and based on fact. On the other hand, the connotative meanings of a word are often very *personal,* and are likely to vary from individual to individual.

Consider the word 'home'. The *denotative* meaning of 'home', given in the dictionary, is 'a place where one lives'. Notice that this simple definition is completely neutral: it does not indicate anything about homes beyond the fact that people live in them.

When we think of the *connotations* of the word 'home', however, the emotional associations are strong. Most people associate 'home' with comfort, food, and rest – a kind of refuge from the world. Therefore, the connotations of the word 'home' are generally positive.

However, for certain unfortunate individuals, the word 'home' would *not* conjure up positive associations. As a matter of fact, bad conditions at home, especially physical abuse, is the most common reason why adolescents run away from home, and become involved in gangsterism.

To reinforce the language point: connotations are emotional, subjective and personal, and are far more difficult to 'pin down' than denotations.

Words with strong emotional connotations can be described as emotive. People use emotive language to express – or to try to arouse – certain feelings. It is important to be able to recognize emotive language and how it works. If we do not, we may be manipulated into unwise behaviour by any individual deliberately using emotive language to serve particular selfish ends. Such manipulators can be found in the media, in advertising, and in politics. These manipulators may use language in calculated ways to arouse emotions, change perceptions, and persuade us to act in the way they desire. Emotive language can thus sometimes control us without our fully realizing it.

TRANSLATING WORDS FROM ONE LANGUAGE TO ANOTHER

Another interesting semantic problem is that there is no simple, one-to-one relationship of meaning between word and object. We tend to accept unquestioningly that a particular word stands for a particular thing, and assume that the same relationships between words and objects exist in all languages. This is not so. As Cook remarks: 'Words are not coins you exchange from one language to another according to a fixed exchange rate'.[1]

Words have nuances, or subtle gradations of meaning. Some languages recognize shades of meaning that other languages ignore. For example, languages vary slightly in how they divide up the colours in which their speakers see the world. The English 'brown' does not correspond exactly to the colour denoted by the French 'brun'. So Cook[2] is not exaggerating when he says that 'learning a second language can literally mean seeing the world in a different way'.

Cook gives the example of the word 'pub'[3], which, he points out, corresponds to nothing in any country other than in the United Kingdom. There is a big variety of tourist bars mistakenly called 'pubs' all over the world. You may have noticed that these days in our own country, the word 'tavern' is being used instead of the word 'shebeen'.

However, the word 'tavern' calls to mind either the English inn or pub of former times, or a restaurant or 'taverna' you would expect to find in a European country such as Greece. These associations are very different from the South African associations attached to the word 'shebeen'. In our view, *shebeen* and *tavern* are not semantic equivalents. But, with continued usage, they may eventually become so, as the connotations of the word 'tavern' change. As we have stressed, language is dynamic, and meanings change over time.

Do you think that for a London businessman the word 'taxi' conjures up the same concept as it does for South Africans? A London taxi is known as a 'black cab', or a 'George' (from George and Dragon/ wagon), or an 'Andy' (from Andy McNab/cab). It is a black saloon car, which usually takes one or two passengers at a time to individual destinations. For most South Africans, a 'taxi' (also known as a 'Zola Budd', a 'Mary Decker', and a 'half-a-loaf') is of the minibus variety usually packed to capacity, which races along well-recognized main routes and into rural areas. The South African taxi industry is unique, with a background and character different from the taxis that serve London commuters.

If you think back to the issue we discussed in Chapter 3: whether language influences thought, you will probably be able to relate these ideas about the meaning of words to that debate. It certainly seems to support the Sapir-Whorf theory that language (in this case vocabulary) determines the way we perceive the world around us.

Chisanga and Kamwangamalu[4] have explored the translation of words from African languages into English, and have demonstrated how difficult it is to do this satisfactorily. The problems arise from the fact that language cannot be separated from its cultural context. The word 'lobola' for instance, is usually translated into English as 'dowry'. However, as they point out, this translation is extremely misleading for a number of reasons. One reason is that it is the bridegroom and not the bride who must bring the *lobola* price (money and other property) – not to the bride, but to the bride's parents. Another reason is that should the bridegroom die, the bride will be 'inherited' by the bridegroom's brother or any designated member within the bridegroom's family. Also, should the bride prove to be barren, the bridegroom can claim one of the bride's sisters to become his wife and bear him children. If the word *lobola* is translated simply and misleadingly as 'dowry', all the important and complex social and traditional meanings associated with *lobola* in African culture are lost.

The same researchers discuss how the vocabulary relating to family and family relationships differs between African languages and English. The concept of kinship is so much more complex and important in African cultures than in Western culture, that it is very difficult to translate words like 'sister' with any degree of accuracy. In many African cultures 'sister' can mean not only 'female sibling', as it does in English, but also 'mother's sister's female child', 'father's brother's female child', and 'father's other wife's female child'. If a speaker wants to convey the English meaning of 'sister', he or she will have to say: 'I went to see my sister, *same father, same mother*'. Thus, the whole socio-cultural context of certain words has to be taken into account in order to understand such words properly.

CONTEXT AND MEANING

The examples discussed above all involve cross-cultural translation, which are obviously complicated by factors specific to particular cultures. Naturally, misunderstandings will arise if translators are not informed about the values and practices of the cultures concerned. We have illustrated how important it is to understand the cultural context when trying to establish meaning.

However, even leaving aside situations involving different cultures, the importance of context in understanding meaning cannot be overstressed. 'Context' in this sense refers to the text of which a particular word forms a part.

To demonstrate how the meaning of words can never be explained in isolation, let us consider the word 'conviction' as an example. What do you understand this word to mean? Could you explain the word on its own – without a context? If not, why not?

It would be impossible for anyone to explain the meaning of 'conviction' without providing a context for the word first. This is because *the context will determine the meaning*.

Now read the two sentences below in which it is used, and reflect on how the context changes the meaning:

1 The prosecutor succeeded in obtaining the *conviction* of the rapist.

Here the word 'conviction' occurs in a context relating to crime and the criminal justice system. This context tells us that 'conviction' means that the accused was *found guilty* as charged.

Now consider the meaning of 'conviction' in the second sentence:

2 The trainer's *conviction* that they would win motivated the team to play their hardest.

In the second sentence, the context is one of a sports competition and the *belief* in a particular team. In this context, the word 'conviction' takes on a completely different meaning: a state of mind and a strong feeling of confidence and certainty.

Without realizing it, we all use *context* all the time to help us work out meaning in our daily interactions. This is an essential part of understanding the language we read and hear around us all day.

Activity 1 Context and meaning

1   Explain the difference in meaning of the highlighted words as they are used in each of the following pairs of sentences:

(a)   The *intelligence* of the child was evident in his advanced mathematical ability.
We received military *intelligence* that troops were sent to the border region.

(b)   Mix one measure of milk powder to three *measures* of water.
The government took strong *measures* to stop the spread of the disease.

2   Now make up two sentences of your own in which you use the word 'patient' in two completely different contexts, so as to bring out the differences in meaning.

(Compare your answers with those suggested at the end of this book.)

WORDS AND GRAMMAR

When learning a language it is not enough to learn the vocabulary. Apart from having a 'mental dictionary', we need to have a 'mental grammar' – an understanding of the internal structure of words, and how words are related to one another in sentences so as to produce meaning.

IDENTIFYING THE UNITS OF LANGUAGE: MORPHEMES

We may think that words are the smallest meaningful units of language that can exist. However, words are made up of even smaller *parts* that have meaning on their own.

Look at the differences between the following pairs of English words:

book and *books*
work and *worked*
kind and *kindly*
approve and *disapprove*

You can see that there is a difference in meaning between the two members of each pair of words. In each case, this difference in meaning is signalled by the addition of a *letter* or a *pair* or *group of letters*: *-s* in the first, *-ed* in the second, *-ly* in the third and *dis-* in the fourth. These letters, or pairs or groups of letters, cannot be used as independent words on their own, but they do have *meaning* on their own. They are obviously important *parts* of the words in which they are used, as they bring about a change in meaning.

We could therefore say that the smallest units in our study of words and grammar are all those *parts of words*, consisting of single letters (or pairs or groups of letters), that have *meaning on their own*. We call these word parts 'morphemes'. A morpheme is the smallest meaningful element into which words can be divided. The word 'meaningful' is important: a part of a word must carry or affect *meaning* to qualify as a morpheme.

Not all words can be divided up: consider the words *yes* and *no*. Here are some more examples of English words that cannot be divided up:

this, that, why, the, are, was, and *there.*

These words consist of a single morpheme, in other words, of a single, meaningful element, such as *yes*. Most words, however, consist of one or more basic morphemes, together with one or more *affixes*. We can divide such words into their parts or *constituent morphemes.*

In each case there will be a *basic* morpheme, such as the morpheme 'appear' in the example 'disappearance'. The affixes attached to the basic morphemes may be *prefixes* (placed in front of the basic morpheme) or *suffixes* (placed after the basic morpheme). In the case of 'disappearance', *dis-* is the prefix and *-ance* is the suffix.

We have mentioned that morphemes carry meaning. For example, the English prefix *dis-* in 'disappearance' expresses a negative meaning. However, we can also use morphemes to create grammatical changes in words. The morpheme *-ance* changes the word from a verb (disappear) to a noun (disappearance).

Let's look again at the example of the words 'book' and 'books' used before. The basic morpheme 'book' can be a noun, in which case the suffix *-s* expresses a plural meaning. Or the word 'book' can be a verb (meaning to *reserve* something), in which case the suffix *-s* expresses the third person singular.

What has happened in these two cases? No *new* words have been formed from the basic morpheme 'book'. The suffix *-s* in each case has been used to show how the word functions in a sentence, or to express 'grammatical contrasts'. In the case of the noun 'books', *-s* expresses the contrast between singular and plural, and in the case of the verb 'books', *-s* expresses the contrast between the third person singular and the other forms of the verb 'book' (*I book, you book,* and so on).

Now think about the word 'booking', a noun meaning *reservation*. This word also contains the basic morpheme 'book', together with the suffix *-ing*. This suffix changes the verb 'book' into a noun, creating, in effect, a *new word.*

You could now practise dividing the words below into their constituent morphemes. Give the meaning of each morpheme.

Activity 2 Constituent morphemes

Divide the words in the list into their constituent morphemes. Consider how these different morphemes change the meaning of the words. The first one has been done for you as an example:

1 *provides*
   provides = basic morpheme *provide* + suffix *-s* expressing third person singular of the verb
2 *elements*
3 *irregular*
4 *clearer*
5 *worthy*
6 *impossible*
7 *cheapest*
8 *uninteresting*

(You will find suggested answers at the end of this book.)

TWO TYPES OF MORPHOLOGY

In English, we add prefixes and suffixes to basic morphemes to make them function in two different ways: to express grammatical contrasts ('inflectional morphology'), or to create new words ('derivational morphology'). Derivational morphology is also called 'lexical morphology', because it produces new words or lexical items.

Inflectional morphology – grammar

'Inflections' refer to those morphemes that are used to change the grammatical meaning of words. To return to a previous example, the morpheme *-s* that changed the singular noun 'book' into the plural noun 'books', is an 'inflectional morpheme'. In English we make use of some inflections, as we have seen, but not nearly as many as are used in Latin or in some other languages.

One important point about the inflections of English is that they all take the form of suffixes, in other words, they are all *word-endings* or affixes attached to the ends of words.

In the list below you will find some of the most important inflections in the English language. You will see that they are all suffixes.

Inflections

1 **Noun plural** (for example *-s*)   as in *books*

2 **Possessive case** (for example *-'s*)   as in *the student's* (card)

3 **Third person singular of verbs** (for example *-s*) as in (the student) *reads*

4 **Past tense** (for example *-ed*)   as in (she) *worked*

5 **Contracted negative** (for example *-n't*)   as in (she) *didn't*

6 **Contracted verbs** (for example *-'re*)   as in *you're* (wrong)

7 **The *-ing* form of the verb,** or the **present participle**   as in *reading*

8 **The *-ed* form of the verb,** or the **past participle**   as in *worked*

9 **The *-er* comparison form** of the adjective   as in *brighter*

10 **The *-est* comparison form** of the adjective   as in *brightest*

Derivational/lexical morphology – word formation

Here we look at ways in which speakers of English use prefixes and suffixes to form new words. The list of such prefixes and suffixes is extremely long, and a list of possible examples would be a great deal longer. We provide just a few examples so that you are aware of how this process works in English.

Prefixes used to form new words

Negation (an indication of the negative)
Examples: *non-* as in *non-smoker*
             un- as in *unhappy*
             in- as in *invisible*
             im- as in *impossible*

Reversal (an indication of changing something back to its original state)
Examples: *de-* as in *defrost* or *detoxify*
             dis- as in *disprove*

Disparagement (an indication that something has little value or is faulty)
Example: *mal-* as in *malnutrition*
             dys- as in *dyslexia* or *dysfunctional*

Size or degree (an indication of size, or of relative importance)
Examples: *mini-* as in *miniskirt*
             mega- as in *megabyte*
             sub- as in *subnormal*; *super-* as in *supernatural*

Orientation (an indication of direction)
Examples: *counter-* as in *counteract*; *retro-* as in *retrospect*
             ex- as in *expel*

Location and distance (an indication of moving or transmitting something across distance)
Examples: *trans-* as in *transplant*
             tele- as in *television*

Time and order (an indication of time (before/after), and of redoing something)
Examples: *pre-* as in *preschool* and *premature*
             post- as in *postnatal*
             re- as in *rewrite*

Number (an indication of quantity)
Examples: *bi-* as in *bicycle* and *bilingual*
             quad- as in *quadruplets*
             multi- as in *multilingual*

We use suffixes in many ways in English to form new words.

Suffixes used to form new words

Forming abstract nouns

Examples: *-ism* as in *idealism*
-ure as in *pleasure*
-dom as in *freedom*
-tion as in *occupation*

Forming concrete nouns

Examples: *-eer* as in *engineer*
-ment as in *pavement*

Forming adverbs

Example: *-wise* as in *clockwise*
-ly as in *quickly*

Forming verbs

Examples: *-en* as in *deafen* or *broaden*
-ize as in *rubberize*

Forming adjectives from nouns

Example: *-an* as in *republican*
-ful as in *useful*

Forming nouns from verbs

Examples: *-er* as in *writer, runner* or *lover*
-ation as in *plantation*
-al as in *arousal*

Forming nouns from adjectives

Example: *-ness* as in *kindness*
-ism as in *nationalism*

Forming adjectives from nouns

Examples: *-less* as in *careless*
-ful as in *youthful*
-ish as in *foolish*

> **Forming adjectives from verbs**
> Examples: -*able* as in *washable* or *affordable*
> -*y* as in *runny*

Morpheme problems

It is not always easy to divide a word into its parts. For example, the word *foot* consists of only one morpheme, and so does the word *feet*, but *feet* is the plural form of *foot*. There is no distinct plural morpheme in the word *feet* as there is in the word *horses*, for example.

MORE WORD-FORMATION PROCESSES IN ENGLISH

We have discussed the ways in which we use prefixes and suffixes to form new words (lexical derivation). There are also other ways to form new words in English.

Compounding

Two words are added together to form one:
shackdweller; earring; password; babysit; worldwide

Coining

New words are coined to name new objects or phenomena:
e-mail; skyjack.

Borrowing

Words are borrowed from other languages:
indaba (Zulu); *lapa* (Sotho); *dagga; gogga* (Khoikhoi); *samoosa* (Indian); *trek; braai; apartheid* (Afrikaans); *creche; salon* (French); *spaghetti* (Italian); *macho; bizarre* (Spanish); *kamikaze* (Japanese); *kindergarten* (German).

Conversion

A word may change its class without changing its form:

* *The host* (noun) becomes *to host* (verb) as in:
  The President *hosted* a dinner for the delegates.

- *The showcase* (noun) becomes *to showcase* as in:
  The festival will *showcase* the talents of local musicians.

- *Up* (preposition) as in *we climbed up the stairs* becomes a verb as in:
  The government will *up* the price of petrol.

Note that the new words we form by conversion eventually become accepted items of vocabulary, and unremarkable in any way.

Here are two examples:
1 There was a time when the word 'access' was almost always used as a noun: 'This gate provides *access* to the minister's residence.' We now use 'access' more and more as a verb: 'To *access* this computer program, you need a password.'
2 Teenagers these days use the word 'party' not only as a noun: 'We are having a *party* on Saturday', but also as a verb: 'We are going to *party* all night'.

Blending

We merge two words into each other:
forex from 'foreign' and 'exchange'
infomercial from 'information' and 'commercial'
educare from 'educate' and 'care'
emoticon from 'emotion' and 'icon'

Clipping

We shorten words:
flu from 'influenza'
ad or *advert* for 'advertisement'
exam for 'examination'
fax for 'facsimile'

Acronyms

We form words from the initial letters of words in sequence, which make up a name or an idea:
Aids from 'Acquired Immune Deficiency Syndrome'
ESCOM from 'Electricity Supply Commission'

Activity 3 Word-formation processes

Identify the word-formation processes we use to produce the words in italics:

1 The novel about the *plane* crash could be described as *faction*.
2 The new *PANSALB website* is working well.
3 The children presented the teacher with a *bouquet*.
4 *Disagreement* flared up at the gathering in the *dorp*.
5 *'Phone* me on my *cell* this evening.
6 *NEPAD* aims to bring stability to the region.
7 We are going to *party* all night.
8 The treatment of patients in the *rehab* centre was *inhumane*.
9 When the money vanished, people started to *finger* the treasurer.
10 The protesters started to *toyi-toyi* outside the *courtroom*.

(You will find suggested answers at the end of this book.)

WORDS AND SENTENCES

In this chapter so far we have considered the grammatical structure of words. We now look at the next level of grammatical structure: 'sentences'. In order to be able to produce meaningful utterances we have to know how to fit words together to form sentences. We shall consider the relationships between words and the patterns and structures into which they fit. These patterns and structures are *essential* to grammar.

At this point we should pause and clarify exactly what the general term 'grammar' means.

Crystal[5] gives two meanings of the term 'grammar'. The first is: 'the study of sentence structure, especially with reference to syntax and morphology'. The second is: 'a systematic account of the rules governing language in general'.

Notice that the word 'rules' appears in the second definition. In what sense is it being used?

Crystal is careful to point out that 'the rules of a generative grammar are not to be confused with the prescriptive "rules" that tell us whether we are right or wrong to use a particular construction. Generative rules have no such implication of social correctness. They are objective descriptions of grammatical patterns that occur'.[6]

The term 'generative grammar', used in the above definition, conveys the fact that we can combine words in an infinite number of different ways to generate new sentences. This important property of language, called 'productivity', makes it possible for speakers to produce an endless number of new sentences.

CONTENT AND STRUCTURE WORDS

When we examine how words 'work' in sentences, we find that words fall into two broad categories; 'structure' and 'content' words.

Content words

Content words are items of vocabulary, such as nouns, verbs, adjectives, and adverbs that can be looked up in a dictionary. They are so numerous as to be uncountable. Examples are 'car', 'bomb', 'explode', 'loudly' and 'fateful'. We produce new content words all the time to name new inventions and phenomena. The rapid development of technology alone ensures that we have to keep on creating words to name new objects and concepts.

Structure words

We use structure (or function) words to provide the framework or 'glue' that holds each part of a sentence together. Structure words are much more limited in number than content words. Examples are articles (or determiners): *a*; *the*; *that*; prepositions: *in* and *of*; pronouns: *he* and *it*; and conjunctions: *and* and *which*. Unlike content words, we cannot invent structure words at will because this would mean having to change the grammatical rules of the language.

If we wanted to make a sentence out of the string of content words named above, we would have to position them within a framework of structure words (printed in italics in the sentence below):

The car bomb exploded loudly *on that* fateful day.

We can illustrate the difference between structure and content words using substitution tables. Study the following sentences, and then make up one or two sentences of your own using the framework below.

By doing this, you will be exploiting the property of *productivity* of language: you could make up an endless number of sentences by substituting different content words.

Structure	Content	Content	Structure	Content	Content
The	farmer	ploughed	the	vast	lands.
A	donkey	pulled	a	heavy	cart.
Some	people	enjoy	these	hectic	routines.

This little exercise may give the impression that it is the content words that supply all the meaning in a sentence. However, the way a sentence is structured is also crucial to meaning. Look at the arrangement of words in the following two questions:

How old is Peter?
How is old Peter?

You will notice that these brief utterances use the same four words. But switching the position of two of the words alters the meaning completely. 'How old is Peter?' relates to Peter's *age*, while 'How is old Peter?' relates to his *health*. Changing the order of the words creates crucial grammatical differences, which affect meaning.

Consider another example of the way we use grammar to change the meaning of the same four words in each of these sentences:

He only reprimanded her.
He reprimanded her only.

In the first sentence, the meaning concerns the *degree* of his reaction. It is implied is that he did not punish her any more severely than merely giving her a reprimand. The second sentence relates to the *object* of his reprimand. It is implied that he could have punished others as well, but he limited his action to her alone.

As we have mentioned, it is only useful to have vocabulary if we know how to use it in statements, questions, or other utterances. To take some examples of words used in the sentences above, we could not say, for example, 'the pulled'. The verb 'pulled' must take a subject and an object – somebody or something has to *do the pulling* and somebody or something has to *be pulled*. Similarly, it would be grammatically impossible to say: 'they enjoyed the hectic'. 'Hectic' is an adjective that must be linked to a noun to be meaningful. To be able to use language grammatically we need to know how words 'behave' together in sentences.

This discussion leads us naturally into a consideration of another aspect of grammar: parts of speech, or 'word classes'.

WORD CLASSES

Earlier, we used some sentences to demonstrate the difference between content and structure words. Look at the same table again, but this time read the columns downwards.

The	farmer	ploughed	the	vast	lands.
A	donkey	pulled	a	heavy	cart.
Some	people	enjoy	these	hectic	routines.

You will notice that all the words in the individual columns are similar 'parts of speech', or belong to the same 'word class' (for example: determiners, nouns, verbs, or adjectives). The words in each *column* function in the same way as one another in the sentences of which they form a part.

The word class to which a word belongs is determined by its 'grammatical function' in context. The same word can belong to a variety of word classes depending on the way it is used in each case. Look at the following sentences. Which word class does the word 'farm' belong to in each sentence?

The *farm* produced an excellent crop.
They decided to *farm* potatoes.
Farm life is healthier than city life.

Clearly, 'farm' is being used as a *noun* in the first sentence, and a *verb* in the second. In the third example, it functions as an *adjective*, describing life.

It is impossible to know what part of speech a word is (or to which word class a word belongs) if we do not know the *function* of the word in its context. Think of a word like 'shop'. Only context will show if the word is being used as a *noun*: 'She walked to the *shop*'; a *verb*: 'She went to *shop* for clothes', or an *adjective:* '*Shop* assistants need to be polite'.

From the time we are in primary school, we are taught parts of speech or word classes by means of simple definitions. 'A noun is a name of a person, place or thing'; 'a verb is a 'doing word''; 'an adjective describes a noun'; 'an adverb modifies a verb'; and so on. Using these conventional definitions, attempt the following exercise.

Activity 4 Word classes

Make up sentences of your own in which you use each of the following words as a *noun*, a *verb*, and an *adjective*:

mark
paint
bottle

(You will find suggested answers at the end of this book.)

Activity 5 Recognizing word classes

Consider the way the word 'back' has been used in each of the following sentences, and identify its word class according to its function in context:

1 When lifting the rock, he hurt his *back*.
2 Please *back* our efforts to raise money for the school library.
3 Give *back* her doll at once.
4 The intruder entered through the *back* door.

(You will find suggested answers at the end of this book.)

Consider the following newspaper headline:

Aircraft crashes

What would you expect to read about in the report that follows this headline?

The probable expectation might be of an accident report in which a particular aeroplane has crashed. In this interpretation, 'aircraft' is assumed to be a *noun*, and 'crashes' a *verb*.

However, the first part of the report that actually followed this headline appears below:

Aircraft crashes

JOHANNESBURG – Aircraft crashes in South Africa ended the '90s at the same level as they began, after an increase in mid-decade.

Figures released by the Civil Aviation Authority show that accidents investigated numbered 152 in 1990 and 153 in 2000.

Pretoria News

When seen in context, we find that the headline introduced a report about the number of aviation accidents that took place in South Africa over a decade. Therefore the report deals with aircraft crashes in a general way. The reader should interpret 'aircraft' as a noun that is used as an *adjective*, and 'crashes' as a *noun*.

This may seem an insignificant example, but it demonstrates how we can use words in *ambiguous* and misleading ways. The ambiguity arises here because at first we do not know the *function* of the two words concerned. Only after reading the report are we able to adjust our interpretation of the headline, and recognize the intended word classes of the words 'aircraft' and 'crashes'. As word classes are determined by their grammatical functions, such a headline could put us into a grammatical 'catch 22' situation.

The following child's riddle provides another example of the way we can use grammar to change the meaning of words:

If you saw a *giant wave*, would you
1   run away from the beach as fast as possible? or
2   wave back?

Notice how central the word classes of 'giant' and 'wave' are to the way we understand the question. Our selection of word classes would dictate which answer we would choose. If you understand 'giant' as an *adjective* meaning 'huge', and 'wave' as a *noun* meaning 'a large movement of water', you would select **1** as your answer.

However, if you understand 'giant' as a *noun* meaning an enormous mythological creature, and 'wave' as a *verb* meaning to move the hand in greeting, you would select the second answer.

Activity 6 Selecting word classes

Consider the two different ways in which the phrase 'The poor bear …' has been developed into two sentences:
1   *The poor bear* crouched in the back of the cage.
2   *The poor bear* many hardships because they cannot afford comfort.

What are the word classes of 'poor' and 'bear' in each of the sentences above? How does your understanding of the meaning of the words 'poor' and 'bear' change according to their function within each sentence?

(Compare your answers with the suggested answers at the end of the book.)

Language is a complex animal, and the *functions* of the different word classes are not always easy to identify. For instance, simple definitions, such as 'a noun is a name of a person, place or thing'; 'a verb is a 'doing word'; and so on, have only limited value. They are oversimplified and thus often unsatisfactory. It is often difficult to match *grammatical function* with the *meaning* of actual words. For example, consider the sentence:

There *was* a loud *explosion* in the factory.

In this sentence, the word 'explosion' has the grammatical function of a *noun*, while 'was' functions as the *verb* in the sentence. However, when we think of the *meaning* of the word 'explosion', we visualize a sudden, forceful release of energy – by no means a static occurrence or phenomenon. Thus 'explosion' seems much closer to the definition of a *verb*, which is supposed to be the part of speech that denotes action.

Similarly, the *verb* in the above sentence, 'was', does not really conjure up the idea of action. It is far less dynamic in meaning than the *noun* 'explosion'.

As another example of the same sort of anomaly, consider the following sentence:

The patient *underwent* a general anaesthetic.

Here the word 'underwent' functions as the *verb* in the sentence. We are talking about undergoing an 'anaesthetic' as though it is something the patient *did*, when in fact the patient is unconscious and lying down in a totally passive state.

Consider one more common example that causes confusion:

Laughing is life's best medicine.

Again, it is the word 'laughing' that conjures up the idea of action, yet it functions as a *noun* in this sentence. 'Is' is the verb in the sentence, yet 'is' seems to be far less dynamic in meaning than 'laughing'. Young learners could not be blamed for identifying 'laughing' as 'the doing word' in this sentence.

Grammatical categories such as word classes are not always logical or easy to explain. Definitions of grammatical classes do not always correspond with meanings. Teachers who become impatient with learners who struggle with grammatical categorization would do well to bear such examples in mind. Remember that grammatical categorization is a set of useful but simple rules we apply to try to explain the numerous and diverse ways words can work together. Language, in its richness and diversity, cannot always be contained by rules of grammar.

SUMMARY

In this chapter, we have dealt with the following main points:

- The relationship between words and meaning is complex.
- The meaning of words must take socio-cultural contexts into account.
- Context determines meaning.
- Words may be divided into smaller units of meaning, called morphemes.
- Inflectional morphology is the study of affixes which are added to the end of words to indicate grammatical changes.
- Derivational (or lexical) morphology is the study of affixes that are added to words to create new words.
- English has several different word-formation processes.
- Grammar is the study of sentence structure and a systematic account of the rules governing language in general.
- Generative grammar describes the process whereby words can be combined in an infinite number of different ways to generate new sentences.
- Words may either be content words or structure words.
- The grammatical function of a word in its context determines its word class and meaning.
- Word classes are not always simple to define.

GLOSSARY

Here is a list of some important terms used in this chapter. Fill in the missing definitions, and add other terms and definitions if you wish.

semantics _____

_____

denotation _____

_____

connotation _____

_____

emotive language _____

_____

morpheme _____

_____

inflectional morphology _____

_____

derivational (or lexical) morphology _____

_____

word-formation processes _____

_____

word classes _____

_____

grammar _____

_____

generative grammar _____

_____

ENDNOTES

1   COOK, V. 1991. *Second language learning and language teaching*, p. 38. London: Edward Arnold.

2   Ibid., p. 39.

3   Ibid., p. 38.

4   CHISANGA, T. AND KAMWANGA-MALU, N. M. 1997. 'Owning the other tongue: the English language in southern Africa' in *Multilingual and multicultural development*, Vol. 18. No. 2.

5   DAVID CRYSTAL. 1987. *The Cambridge Encyclopedia of Language*, p. 422. Cambridge: Cambridge University Press.

6   Ibid., p. 97.

9 What makes language coherent?

CHAPTER OUTLINE

In this chapter we consider what is meant by 'discourse'. We will be examining what gives a text cohesion and coherence.

LEARNING OUTCOMES

By the end of this chapter you should have the following knowledge, skills, values, and attitudes:

Knowledge

You should understand
- the meaning of the term *discourse*
- the meaning of the terms *cohesion* and *coherence*, and
- the meaning of the term *schemata* and how these affect comprehension.

Skills

You should be able
- to recognize cohesive ties in a piece of discourse and understand how these function, and
- to understand what makes discourse coherent.

Values and attitudes

You should develop
- understanding and respect for the various factors that influence the ability to interpret language.

INTRODUCTION

So far we have dealt with *words* and *sentences*. We now move on to consider *discourse*.

What does *discourse* mean?

Traditionally, the study of language has been concerned mainly with the construction of sentences. Lately, however, there has been a growing interest in the way sentences work in sequence and in combination; to produce cohesive, coherent stretches of language.

> **Discourse** consists of longer 'stretches' of language, and how these carry meaning in a sustained, comprehensible manner.

The relatively new interest in longer 'chunks' of language is a reminder that language is always spoken or written in a particular context. The interaction of language and social context cannot be properly appreciated if we confine ourselves to the examination of single sentences.

Individual sentences seldom stand alone; they are usually connected to something that was said or written before and will be followed by something else. In this way, they form part of a *larger discourse*.

A crucial principle underlying discourse study is that the sentences that make up a text are related to, and are dependent on, one another. The relationships between the sentences in a text create *cohesion*.

COHESION

The term *cohesion* refers to the 'links' that exist between the individual parts of a text. There is a kind of *mutual dependence* between sentences. The reader (or the listener in the case of spoken language) depends on these links in order to make sense of what is written or said. As is true of so much in our use of language, we take these connections for granted. They have to be pointed out before we become consciously aware of them.

There are several types of links or 'cohesive factors' in discourse. The most important ones are listed and are briefly explained below.

● Co-reference

This term refers to the way certain words refer to certain previously mentioned words in the text to convey meaning. For example, in the sentence: 'Jill wrote the exam and she passed it', we only know who the 'she' in the sentence refers to by referring back to 'Jill', and we only know what 'it' refers to by referring back to 'exam'. This very common cohesive link is known as 'pronoun co-reference'.

There are other types of co-reference too. In the sentence: 'I visited the Drakensberg in my childhood, but only returned *there* in middle age', the word 'there' refers back to 'the Drakensberg'. 'There' is not a pronoun – it is an adverb. Nevertheless it cannot be understood without referring to a previously named item in the text.

• Conjunctive relations (or logical connectors)

These are the linking words such as *and, but, when, because, although, so,* and *finally,* which help to give a text logical and chronological (time) structure. The conjunctive relations in the following paragraph have been italicized to illustrate how they contribute towards cohesion:

> Lucy had *always* wanted a puppy for a pet, *so when* she saw puppies in the pet shop, she nagged her father to buy her one. *But* he refused, *and* she was broken-hearted. *Eventually* he relented *and as a result* she was a happy child *again.* She loved her new companion.

Conjunctive relations, or logical connectors, convey connections between events, time, contrasts, and results.

• Ellipsis

When a piece of structure is omitted, it may be understood nevertheless. In the 'Lucy and the puppies' paragraph above, one sentence begins: 'But he refused…' (to do what?) The words: 'to buy her a puppy' are omitted, but we understand what is meant all the same.

• Repeated forms

This refers to the repetition of certain words or structures. The words of a Calvin Klein advertisement read: 'Be hot. Be cool. Just be.' Such repetitive sentence structures are often used to increase the effect of a text.

• Comparison

Comparison is used to link sentences. For example: 'The children were bony and thin. *Even thinner* were their cows'. Here, 'even thinner' cannot be properly understood without the previous statement about the thin children.

• Substitution

One feature may replace a previous expression. For example, 'Do you think she is honest? I think *so.*' Here, 'so' refers to the belief in her honesty. In the Lucy example given above, the word 'one' in 'to buy her one' substitutes for 'puppy'. 'Her new companion' is another way of referring to 'puppy', so is also an example of substitution.

• Lexical relationships

When there is a close relationship between words of consecutive sentences, the sentences are 'lexically linked'. These relationships include 'synonyms' (closely associated words) and words that fall into the same lexical field.

Consider the following sets of words:
1 stove   spatula   kettle   egg-beater   frying-pan   grater
2 book   tree   pillow   bath   cloud   door   computer

All the words in set **1** refer to items used in the kitchen for the preparation of food. We can thus say that they fall into the same 'lexical field'. The words in the second set, however, have nothing in common with one another, and so are lexically unrelated.

Using the 'Lucy' example again, 'puppies', 'pet', and 'pet shop' are lexically linked. We could call this series of words a 'lexical chain'. There can be more than one lexical chain in a piece of discourse.

Other features that can contribute to cohesion are *verb tenses, person, voice*, and things like the *length of sentences, sound,* and *rhythm.* In fact, *any feature that makes the parts of a piece of discourse belong together contributes to cohesion.*

Text cohesion in practice

Although knowing terms such as 'pronoun co-reference' and 'conjunctive relations' is useful when discussing cohesive links, it is more important that you understand how these links actually 'work' in the text. We would rather you were able to *demonstrate* how cohesive devices help to create cohesion, than be able to use these terms in a meaningless way to show that you have 'learned' them by rote. Do not get bogged down in terminology for its own sake. The aim is to *develop the skill of recognizing* the different cohesive links and *understand* how these function in their context.

Let us look at another example of cohesion, this time in a shortened extract from a newspaper text:

An African icon turns 70

SEVENTY YEARS YOUNG, seventy years beautiful. Miriam Makeba's birthday today is yet another moment to honour the graceful empress of African song.

Our greatest international star has been famous for at least 50 years, and has never lost her lustre.

Much like icon Elizabeth Taylor, who turned 70 last week, Makeba's cultural significance has only deepened over the years with her social consciousness and ageless ability to entertain.

Pretoria News, 4 March, 2002

There is no particular order in which to find cohesive links. Start with those that stand out most for you in the particular passage. You will spot some cohesive devices immediately, while others will take longer to find. The *lexical links* in this passage struck us first.

Lexical relationships

- Words associated with *time*:
  'seventy years', 'at least 50 years', 'never', 'over the years', and 'ageless'.
  This lexical chain emphasizes the *enduring nature* of Miriam Makeba's talent.

- Words associated with being a *celebrity in show business* form another lexical chain:
  'graceful empress of African song', 'greatest international star', 'famous', 'lustre', 'icon', and 'ability to entertain'.

Repeated forms

- '*Seventy years* young, *seventy years* beautiful'.
  This use of *repetition* is deliberate and creates a pleasing aural effect.

- 'Icon', 'icon':
  Again – repetition is used in the comparison of Miriam Makeba to Elizabeth Taylor.

Ellipsis

- '*[She is]* seventy years young, *[she is]* seventy years beautiful'.
  The words 'she is' are omitted, but we understand that they are implied nonetheless.

Substitution

- Miriam Makeba is referred to as 'the graceful empress of African song', and 'our greatest international star'. These descriptions are different ways of referring back to the same person.

Comparison

- 'Much like icon Elizabeth Taylor ...'
  This direct comparison is such an obvious link that it needs no further explanation.

Conjunctive relations/logical connectors:

- 'Yet another', 'and', 'never', 'much like', 'who', 'with', and 'and'

You may have spotted other cohesive links, or perhaps you emphasized the ones we have listed above in a different way. Do not worry if this is the case. To reiterate, it is important to try to recognize as many as you can, and to understand how they function in the particular piece of discourse.

FINDING COHESIVE LINKS: A PRACTICAL EXERCISE

Now try a practical example of finding cohesive links in a piece of discourse. Take a pencil and mark as many examples of cohesion as you can find in the following passage:

The silent brown river overflowed its banks. Like a crocodile on a slow, solitary hunt it crept up in the night, homing in on its prey. A village that nestled close to the river banks—a pretty place with round chocolate-coloured huts with light cream thatching—lay in its path.

The river flooded the fields around the village and carried chickens and goats away with it. Then it began its assault on the hut that lay closest to its banks. It hesitated momentarily as it slopped against the slightly raised step. Then the sheer weight of the water behind it forced the water relentlessly upwards.

From *Thoko*, by Brenda Munitich[1]

(Ensure that you attempt this exercise on your own before consulting the points listed below.)

Co-reference

'It' and 'its', throughout the passage, refer to 'river'. 'Its' in line 2 refers back to 'crocodile'. 'A pretty place' refers back to 'village'.

Conjunctive relations

'Like', 'that', 'and', 'then', 'that', 'as', and 'then'.

Lexical relationships

- Words associated with water:
  'river', 'overflowed', 'banks', 'river banks', 'flooded', 'banks', 'slopped', and 'water'.

- Words associated with a rural setting:
  'River', 'village', 'huts', 'fields', 'huts', 'thatching', 'chickens', 'goats', and 'hut'.

- Words presenting the river as a danger:
  'Like a crocodile on a slow, solitary hunt it crept up … homing in on its prey'; and 'assault'.

Verb tenses

All the verbs are in the *past tense*, providing a consistent time-frame for the piece, and giving a sense of a continuous narrative.

Activity 1 Finding cohesive links

Examine the following piece of discourse carefully, marking and identifying all the cohesive links you can find.

> Toloki notices that in every shack they visit, the women are never still. They are always doing something with their hands. They are cooking. They are sewing. They are outside scolding the children. They are at the tap drawing water. They are washing clothes. They are sweeping the floor in their shacks, and the ground outside. They are closing holes in the shacks with cardboard and plastic. They are loudly joking with their neighbours while they hang washing on the line. Or they are fighting with the neighbours about children who have beaten up their own children. They are preparing to go to the taxi rank to catch taxis to the city, where they will work in the kitchen of their madams.
>
> Men, on the other hand, tend to cloud their heads with pettiness and vain pride. They sit all day and dispense wide-ranging philosophies on how things should be. With great authority in their voices, they come up with wise theories on how to put the world right. Then at night they demand to be given food, as if the food just walked into the house on its own. When they believe all the children are asleep, they want to be pleasured. The next day they wake up and continue with their empty theories.

From *Ways of dying* by Zakes Mda[2]

(Compare your answers with those suggested at the end of the book.)

PARAGRAPH COHESION

'Paragraph cohesion' is based on the same principles as the cohesion of longer units.

An effective way to demonstrate cohesion is to take the sentences out of the text and to change their order at random. Then try to put them into the correct order again. This forces us to notice the cohesive links we are normally unaware of.

Activity 2 Sequence of sentences

In each of the following two paragraphs, the sentences have been randomly shuffled. Indicate their correct sequence by writing down the sentence numbers in the correct order in each case.

Paragraph 1

1 For one thing, he hated the summer holidays more than any other time of the year.

2 And he also happened to be a wizard.

3 Harry Potter was a highly unusual boy in many ways.

4 For another, he really wanted to do his homework, but was forced to do it in secret, in the dead of night.

From *Harry Potter and the prisoner of Azkaban* by J. K. Rowling

Paragraph 2

1 The trunks of the trees were also dusty.

2 In the bed of the river there were pebbles and boulders, and the water was clear and blue.

3 In the late summer of that year we lived in a house in a village that looked across the river to the mountains.

4 Troops went past the house and down the road, and the dust they raised powdered the leaves of the trees.

Adapted from *A farewell to arms* by Ernest Hemingway

(Compare your answers with those suggested at the end of the book.)

COHERENCE

'Coherence' has to do with the 'logical relationships' between the *ideas* and *concepts* expressed in the discourse. It might help you to understand what 'coherence' means if you think of its opposite: 'incoherence'. If you say that someone is 'incoherent', you mean that what they say makes no sense, perhaps because they are upset, drunk, or physically or mentally ill.

In discussing coherence, Yule refers to the 'meaningful connections' that underlie our understanding of what we read and hear.[3] If these connections do not exist, we try to create them or 'fill the gaps', but if this is not possible, the text remains incoherent.

Consider this example of incoherent discourse.[4] It is amusing *because* it is incoherent:

GROUCHO: *Now listen here. I've got a swell job for you, but first I'll have to ask you a couple of important questions. Now, what is it that has four pair of pants, lives in Philadelphia, and it never rains but it pours?*

CHICO: *Atsa good one. I give you three guesses.*

GROUCHO: *Now, let me see. Has four pair of pants, lives in Philadelphia ... Is it male or female?*

CHICO: *No, I not think so.*

GROUCHO: *Is he dead?*

CHICO: *Who?*

GROUCHO: *I don't know. I give up.*

CHICO: *I give up too. Now I ask you another one. What is it got big black-a moustache, smokes a big black cigar, and is a big pain in the neck?*

GROUCHO: *Now, don't tell me. Has a big black moustache, smokes a big black cigar and is a big pain in the—*

CHICO: *Uh—*

GROUCHO: *Does he wear glasses?*

CHICO: *Atsa right. You guess it quick.*

GROUCHO: *Just for that, you don't get the job I was going to give you.*

CHICO: *What job?*

GROUCHO: *Secretary of War.*

CHICO: *All right, I take it.*

GROUCHO: *Sold!*

It is possible for a text to be cohesive but not coherent. *Coherence* is *more than* just the structural relations between parts of a text. It has to do with the ideas or concepts expressed in the various parts of the text. Crystal states that coherence refers to the fact that 'the concepts and relationships expressed should be relevant to each other'.[5]

Coherent discourse can be clearly understood. It has clear, logical links in the use of language. The clarity of its meaning, or coherence, depends to a large degree on the skills of the speaker or writer, but this is not enough. It also depends on the *background knowledge* and *linguistic knowledge* of the listener or reader.

Consider this hypothetical situation: A stranger goes to a lecture where a very brilliant professor discusses his theory on some aspect of nuclear science. What he says may be perfectly coherent to those members of the audience who are informed in the field, but the stranger, a complete novice, finds the lecturer totally incoherent. The professor's use of language and his knowledge of the subject are not faulty, but what he says is not meaningful to the stranger because the latter lacks background knowledge and an understanding of the terminology used by the professor.

So, coherence is not something that only exists in the language used by the speaker or writer. Obviously, language usage is important, but whether it is understood or not depends on other human and social elements in the communicative situation.

You may remember that in Chapter 6 we discussed *implicatures*, or the way people pick up unstated or implied information in conversation. Some exchanges lack cohesive ties and seem incoherent in themselves, but because the participants have additional knowledge, they are each able to interpret what the other says. Let us consider an example of a conversation between two men:

A: *The dog's barking.*
B: *The neighbours are away.*

These two sentences appear quite unconnected, yet the two men involved make sense to each other.

When A says: 'the dog's barking', he is concerned that this will disturb the neighbours. The neighbours have probably complained before about the noisy dog, so B understands what A is implying. B is able to give him the information he needs to allay his anxiety – that the neighbours have gone away, so it doesn't matter if the dog barks, and A need not worry.

It is clear that factors other than the actual words spoken make this snippet of conversation *coherent* to the parties involved. More than linguistic knowledge is involved here. It is the background knowledge of the people concerned that enables them to fill in the gaps and make sense of what they hear.

BACKGROUND KNOWLEDGE OR SCHEMATA

As we have tried to illustrate, our understanding of what we hear or read does not all come directly from the language itself. A great deal of our ability to interpret the language around us depends on our background knowledge (also known as 'extralinguistic knowledge', because it is information that exists *outside* the language). We all have knowledge structures in our minds that we have built up through experience and stored in our memories. The technical name for these knowledge structures is 'schemata'. (Please note that 'schemata' is the plural form of the word 'schema'.)

When we communicate, we assume vast amounts of *shared* background knowledge. If we are correct in our assumption that our audience shares our knowledge, what we say will be understood, and our verbal interaction will be successful. If, on the other hand, a listener or reader does not share the same background knowledge as us, there will be a breakdown of communication, as happened in the unfortunate case of the stranger listening to the nuclear scientist, given as an example in the previous page.

Our schemata are built up from our own personal experience. Naturally, because of this, different people have different schemata. The differences may be slight, and cause minor misunderstandings, but if the differences are fundamental, major bafflement could result. One of the first things a teacher learns is not to assume that learners have the necessary background knowledge to receive a new teaching point. The first step in a lesson is to build up the necessary schemata to help learners comprehend what is to come.

To sum up this discussion of discourse, let us reconsider the definition we gave earlier:

'Discourse consists of longer 'stretches' of language, and how these carry meaning in a sustained, comprehensible manner'.

To interpret a piece of discourse, we use the text's cohesive elements, to which we add background knowledge of our own. If the text has *cohesion*, and we have the appropriate *schemata*, the discourse will be *coherent* and fully comprehensible.

SUMMARY

In this chapter, we have dealt with the following main points:

- Discourse refers to 'stretches of language' (mutually dependent or linked sentences), which carry meaning.
- In a piece of discourse there are cohesive ties between sentences.
- Linguistic and extralinguistic factors combine to make a text coherent.
- Schemata are knowledge structures carried in the memory which help to make discourse coherent and comprehensible.

GLOSSARY

Here is a list of some important terms used in this chapter. Fill in the missing definitions, and add other terms and definitions.

discourse _____

_____

cohesion _____

_____

co-reference _____

_____

conjunctive relations _____

_____

ellipsis _____

_____

lexical field _____

_____

lexical chain _____

_____

coherence   _____

_____

schema/schemata   _____

_____

ENDNOTES

1 MUNITICH, BRENDA. 1992. *Thoko*, p. 1. Cape Town: Tafelberg.

2 MDA, ZAKES. 1995. *Ways of dying*, p. 164. Cape Town: Oxford University Press.

3 YULE, GEORGE. 1995. *The study of language.* Cambridge low price editions, p. 106-7. Cambridge: Cambridge University Press.

4 AKMAJIAN, ADRIAN ET AL. 1984. *Linguistics: an introduction to language and communication*, p. 419. Cambridge, Massachusetts: The MIT Press.

5 CRYSTAL, DAVID. 1987. *The Cambridge Encyclopedia of Language*, p. 119. Cambridge: Cambridge University Press.

10 How do we analyse discourse?

CHAPTER OUTLINE

So far we have been discussing ideas about language in general, and English in particular. We have also considered the structure of words, sentences, and discourse. In this final chapter, we deal in greater detail with the structure of discourse.

LEARNING OUTCOMES

By the end of this chapter you should have the following knowledge, skill, values, and attitudes:

Knowledge

You should understand
- the meaning of the terms *discourse analysis* and *text analysis*, and
- the way in which language reflects the nature and identity of the writer, and is adapted to the context, the intended audience, and the purpose of the discourse.

Skills

You should be able
- to apply the knowledge described above in analysing different texts.

Values and attitudes

You should develop
- understanding and sensitivity to the factors that influence the different types of discourse produced within different contexts for different audiences and purposes.

INTRODUCTION

We have chosen to end this book with *discourse analysis* because it embraces all aspects of English language study covered so far. Analysing discourse involves recognizing, pointing out, and commenting on all the different aspects of language in a given text that we have discussed in this book. These include the following:

- the *identity* and *characteristics* of the speaker or writer
- the *functions* and *purposes* for which the language is being used
- the *variety* of language being used
- the *connotations* and *emotive power* of the vocabulary
- the *structure* of the words, sentences and paragraphs, and
- the *relations* between them.

Discourse analysis

This term refers to the process of examining the structure of naturally occurring spoken and written language.

Discourse analysis represents the culmination and application of all the knowledge and skills you have acquired in working though this book.

As pointed out in Chapters 8 and 9, words and sentences cannot be discussed in isolation: they occur in particular *contexts*, usually connected to something that was said or written before and often followed by something else. In this way, words and sentences form part of a larger *discourse*.

As mentioned, lately there has been greater interest in studying longer stretches of language, or discourse. In this chapter we discuss techniques of discourse analysis.

What do we mean by the term 'discourse analysis'?

We would like to stress that the *structure* of discourse, whether spoken or written, is the focus of analysis. In discourse analysis, the emphasis is on the *parts*, and the *relationships* between the parts.

DISCOURSE AND TEXT

The entry below is from the *Oxford Advanced Learner's Dictionary*:

discourse *n* **1** [C] (*fml*) a long and serious treatment or discussion of a subject in speech or writing ... **2** [U] (*linguistics*) the use of language in speech and writing in order to produce meaning; language that is studied, usually in order to see how the different parts of a text are connected: *spoken/written discourse* ◊ *discourse analysis*.

The second definition is the one that is relevant for our purposes.

Although some people refer to *discourse* as examples of spoken language, and *text* as examples of written language, the dictionary entry above shows that we can apply the term *discourse* to both *spoken* and *written* communication between people. We use the term *discourse* to refer to both forms of communication. In any case, our present medium (this book) compels us to transcribe all spoken discourse into print, or the *written* form. Thus the analysis of different types of communication will necessarily have to take place through the medium of *text*.

Bear in mind that the notion of 'text' can and often does include a range of visual texts besides the printed word, such as pictures, photographs, images, cartoons, and other graphic devices (such as different print sizes, fonts, layouts, and arrangement of space and colour).

Below is a random list of items. Taking into account the definition of 'text' above, which of these items could be described as a *text*? Which of these could be subjected to discourse analysis?

a joke	a novel
a newspaper article	an advertisement
an academic lecture	a play
an autobiography	an encyclopedia article
a prayer	a political speech
a medical diagnosis	a scientific textbook
a sermon	a comic strip
interior dialogue (private thoughts)	a conversation with your parents
a television show	a political manifesto
a short story	a letter to a friend
a university textbook	a letter to your employer
a poem	your personal diary

The answer is that *ALL* of the above items are texts and can be subjected to discourse analysis.

DISCOURSE/TEXT ANALYSIS

When we attempt discourse analysis, we have to examine a 'chunk' or a 'stretch' of language and discuss its features. How and where do we start?

We would suggest a four-pronged approach. This would involve considering:

1 The *person producing the language* – in other words, the *speaker* or *writer*.
2 The *context* in which the language is produced.
3 The *audience* for whom it is intended.
4 The *purpose* of the language, or what it sets out to achieve.

All the factors listed above will combine to influence the *tone* and *style* of the language used. We will consider tone and style more fully later.

Let us now consider each of the four factors above in turn.

1 Producer of language (speaker or writer)

The identity and characteristics of the speaker or writer will influence the kind of language used. Personal factors would include such things as:

- level of education
- social status
- whether the person speaks English as a primary or additional language
- if English is an additional language, the influence of the primary language
- age
- gender
- personality, values, attitudes, and
- social and political views and position.

The last point may only be revealed through the *implicatures* of the discourse, which have been discussed in Chapter 6. People sometimes speak in a way that *suggests* certain views and assumes that the audience shares these views. If someone tells a sexist joke, for example, they are revealing sexist attitudes and are implying that they think their audience shares these attitudes and will not be offended.

Activity 1 Producer of language (speaker or writer)

Consider the following sentences. What information do they convey about the *identity of the person* who has uttered them? Try to pinpoint which verbal clues you use to help you to arrive at your conclusions.

1   So I says to him if he doesn't watch it, I'll donder him stukkend.
2   The exquisite view filled my soul with rapture.
3   My father she is very sick.
4   The economic indicators on the stock exchange show that the rand is strengthening in relation to other world currencies.
5   Wow! What a great movie!

(Compare your answers with those suggested at the end of the book.)

---

2 Context

Language cannot be separated from its context, because it is a product of context. The notion of *context* entails such factors as:

- historical period (*when* the language occurred)
- region/geographical place (*where* the language occurred), and
- situation (the *circumstances* in which it occurred).

Most of the time, we expect language to be *appropriate* to its context, or the situation in which it is used. For example, there are certain kinds of language that are considered appropriate for religious ceremonies, for classroom interaction, for social gatherings, and for business meetings. Our knowledge of what is suitable for various contexts is called 'pragmatic competence'. We very often apply this knowledge without being consciously aware of it.

Activity 2 Context

What do the following four examples convey about the possible contexts in which they were produced? Try to pinpoint which verbal clues you used to arrive at your conclusions.

1 Avaunt! and quit my sight! Let the earth hide thee!
   Thy bones are marrowless, thy blood is cold;
   Thou hast no speculation in those eyes,
   Which thou dost glare with.
2 Viva! Viva! Freedom to all! Amandla!
3 How do you plead? Guilty or not guilty?
4 Come on, ladies and gentlemen, put your hands together for the singing sensation of the decade!

(Compare your answers with those suggested at the end of the book.)

3 Audience

We talk to different people in different ways. See how a simple greeting – spoken by the same person – can change, depending on the audience.

- Good morning, sir.
- Hi, guys.
- Howzit!
- Good day, how may I help you?
- Hello.

In the case of a written text, the audience refers to the people who read or listen to the text. A writer often knows who these readers are and what they are like. The same message may be written in different ways for different audiences.

Speakers and writers have to take their audiences into account and adapt their language accordingly. The target audience may be described in some of the following terms:

- level of education
- degree of specialization in a particular field
- age, and
- gender.

The speaker or writer may also know or assume the audience's political views.

Activity 3 Audience

What do the following examples convey about the possible *audiences* being addressed?

Try to pinpoint which verbal clues you should use to arrive at your conclusions.

1 Sit down and stop talking at once, unless you want to stay in at break!
2 Pamper yourself with the lingering perfume of creamy *Rosefair* body lotion.
3 In this semester you will learn about different mutations of this specific virus.
4 Go bundu-bashing in a vehicle as rugged and tough as yourself.
5 See you at the stadium on Saturday, my bra.

(Compare your answers with those suggested at the end of the book.)

---

4 Purpose

The purpose can be whatever the producer of the language (speaker or writer) intends to achieve through the discourse. Functions of language were discussed in Chapter 3. Here are seven possible purposes the speaker or writer may wish to achieve in discourse. Any combination of the following is also possible.

To instruct

In writing that is intended to instruct, the word choice will be factual and precise. The sentence structures will include imperative or 'command' verb forms, and will also use sequencing to indicate the correct order in which things ought to be done to achieve a particular outcome.

To inform

When a writer's purpose is to inform, precision will (or should) be the main feature of the writing. This is a case where the effectiveness of the writing can be judged by the outcome: did the reader clearly understand the information provided in the text?

To persuade

Persuasive writing will contain emotive language, in other words, language that is chosen to evoke an emotional reaction on the part of the audience, or to move the audience to action. Advertisers and politicians exploit this type of speech to persuade people to buy a certain product, or to persuade people to vote for a particular political party.

To entertain

Think of possible ways in which a piece of writing can entertain: it may amuse, it may provide beauty, or it may simply be intriguing. In whatever way the speaker/writer entertains, he or she will do so by using language for a purpose beyond merely providing information.

To sell

The seller or advertiser will try to manipulate your emotions in order to make you buy a product. Therefore the purpose of persuading will underlie this discourse. Look at the following example from an advertisement for a holiday destination: 'Imagine a land of thrilling opportunities, exciting destinations where wildlife gracefully roams the majestic, pristine landscape …'. Apart from the liberal use of emotive language, the seller may try to create a sense of urgency by means of exclamations such as: 'Win up to R5 000 with your game card NOW!' or by trying to involve you through asking rhetorical questions like: 'What's nicer than a hot bowl of soup on a chilly day?'

To complain

When someone is so dissatisfied with something that they are moved to complain, their language will probably be emotive, and is likely to express disappointment and/or anger. The complainant may also demand some sort of action or apology for whatever it is they are complaining about.

To satirize

Writers, artists, and comedians often use satire (mockery) to point out faults or to make a social or political comment about a well-known person, topical event or situation. Although the most important point they make may be far from funny, they make use of humour to attract the reader or listener. Such writers or speakers thus entertain or amuse, as well as provoke serious thought.

Activity 4 Purpose

What do the following examples convey about *purpose*?

Try to pinpoint the verbal clues you should use to arrive at your conclusions.

1 Have you heard the one about the Englishman, the Irishman and Van der Merwe?
2 The code for all telephone numbers in the area has changed to 0132.
3 Yesterday I had to wait for more than an hour for my train. This is unacceptable.
4 Do have a doughnut – they are delicious. I got them fresh from the bakery this morning.
5 Open your textbooks at page 32. Please do Activity 15, making sure that you include the points we have been discussing.
6 If you buy one today, you could win the car of your dreams!
7 Cartoon:

Sunday Times, November 11, 2001

(Compare your answers with those suggested at the end of the book.)

We now want to demonstrate how the four main factors listed above – the *speaker/writer; context; audience;* and *purpose* – determine the nature of the resulting discourse. They will combine to influence the *tone* and *style* of the language used.

Tone and *style* are abstract categories, and quite difficult to recognize and define. Here are some things to look for when analysing the tone and style of a piece of discourse:

Tone

Tone has to do with the *feeling* or *attitude* with which a writer or speaker treats a subject and an audience. Tone is very often conveyed by the connotations and emotive power of the vocabulary and expressions chosen. You can ask yourself how the producer of the language *sounds* and *feels* about the audience and the message.

Here are some examples of the kinds of tone that may be found in speech and writing:

- neutral, objective, and matter-of-fact (with a minimum of emotion or feeling)
- personal
- impersonal
- formal
- informal
- sad
- angry
- filled with admiration
- bitter
- anxious
- ironic or sarcastic
- triumphant
- determined
- optimistic

Style

In order to determine style you should consider sentence structures as well as vocabulary and expressions. Here are some things to look out for:

Words

- Are the words long and difficult, or short and simple?
- Are there any foreign (non-English) words?
- Is the vocabulary difficult and intended for a specialist audience, or is it simple enough for a general audience and even children to understand?
- Are there any archaic or old-fashioned words?
- Is there slang associated with any particular group, or 'insider' language known only to a particular group?
- Are there any phonological effects such as rhyme or alliteration?
- Are there any unconventional or taboo words?
- Are the nouns mainly concrete or abstract?
- Are there examples of puns or wordplay?
- Is there any emotive or extreme language? (look at adjectives and adverbs)
- Is the language hyperbolic (exaggerated) or is it understated?
- Are the words literal or figurative? (Is there any use of imagery?)

Sentences

- Are the sentences long or short, simple or complex?
- Do the sentences follow the usual word order of subject followed by verb?
- Are there simple coordinators such as 'and'?
- Are the sentences active or passive?
- Are there exclamations?
- Is there a particular format with sub-sections, or a particular layout involving charts, diagrams, and tables, for example?
- Is the content presented in a list or point form?
- Is there any use of repetition for effect?
- Are there any rhetorical questions?
- Is there a question-and-answer format?

You can use these pointers as a handy checklist to consider closely the words and structures in the text, to help you write an informed discussion of any piece of discourse.

When tackling discourse analysis, you need to begin with the 'end product' and work 'backwards'. In other words, look closely at *what*

Discourse analysis

Remember that all aspects of a text are *interrelated*. There are always *connections* between the particular *language* of the discourse that is created and the *speaker/writer, context, audience,* and *purpose*. All these aspects will affect the *tone* and *style* of the discourse.

you find in the language, and then analyse what this *suggests* about the *speaker/writer, context, audience,* and *purpose*.

TACKLING DISCOURSE ANALYSIS

We are now going to attempt some practical examples of discourse analysis.[1]

We suggest the following strategy:

1 Read the text thoroughly and carefully, as many times as you need, to understand what it is about.

2 With a pencil, mark any feature that stands out for you. Underline and circle significant words and phrases. Use arrows to link things that appear to go together. Jot down brief comments in the margin to explain the things you have marked in the text.

3 Take a blank piece of paper. Draw four columns, and head them: *Speaker/Writer; Context; Audience;* and *Purpose*. In the columns jot down whatever you can find to say about each of these four categories. Refer to the guidelines on pages 200 to 207 in this chapter, to remind yourself of what to look out for.

4 On a separate sheet of paper, make a note of all the *language features* such as words and sentence structures that have influenced your assessment of the four categories above. For example, if you come across the words 'thee' and 'thou', and you think that the text is a sermon delivered in a religious context, write these words down. Keep going back to the text you are analysing, and add to your notes if necessary.

(Remember that when you come to write out your full analysis, you will have to use a number of quotations from the text to substantiate your observations, so make sure you move between our guidelines and the text when making connections.)

5 When you think you have found as many points as you can, use your jottings on the text, in the margins, and in the columns as the 'raw material' of your discourse analysis. Decide on the order of your discussion. You can now start to write out a rough version of your analysis using full sentences and paragraph form.

6 Develop and refine your discussion with further drafts until you are satisfied that you have said everything you want to. Ensure that your final analysis is well constructed and clearly written.

Your approach should be first to recognize what is there, and then suggest a *connection* between the *language* itself and the producer, the context, the audience, and the purpose. In other words, avoid deciding *in advance* what the speaker/writer is like; what the purpose is; and what the audience is like, and looking for clues in the writing to support or even 'prove' your preconceived notions. Instead, you should look closely at *what you find* in the language, and then analyse what this *suggests* about speaker/writer, context, audience, and purpose.

As you can see, the analysis of a piece of discourse is not a quick or simple task. However, if you follow our suggested steps, you should find it challenging, but manageable.

As an example, we are now going to do a discourse analysis of a particular text.

Example 1

This is the closing part of Nelson Mandela's speech to the court at the 'Rivonia Treason Trial', which is reproduced in his autobiography *Long walk to freedom* [2].

> During my lifetime, I have dedicated myself to this struggle of the African people. I have fought against white domination, and I have fought against black domination. I have cherished the ideal of a democratic and free society in which all persons live together in harmony and with equal opportunities. It is an ideal which I hope to live for and to achieve. But if needs be, it is an ideal for which I am prepared to die.

Nelson Mandela's well-known speech to the court at the 'Rivonia Treason Trial' is an example of a *persuasive* text with a *serious tone*. The *speaker* is the leader of a political movement, on trial for what was then a charge carrying the most serious penalties. The *context* is the courtroom at the end of these very serious legal proceedings, and although the words were spoken in this context, they were suitable for, and even intended for, a *general audience*.

(The transcript of a speech represents the written form of a piece of discourse that was intended to be spoken, and can therefore be analysed both as written and as spoken discourse.)

The purpose of this text seems to be mainly persuasive. The specific aim seems to be to persuade the listener or reader to recognize, respect, and understand the speaker's ideals. The speaker uses two important devices found in persuasive writing: emotive language, and repetition.

There are several emotive words that suggest the speaker's high ideals and aspirations. The word 'dedicated' suggests that the speaker has given and devoted everything he has had to the cause with which has identified himself. The word 'cherished' suggests how precious and highly valued the speaker's ideals are. The adjectives 'democratic' and 'free', and the noun 'harmony', are further examples of emotive language with positive connotations, and suggest the positive values for which the speaker has fought.

Another aspect of the text that suggests its persuasive purpose is the use of repetition. The clause 'I have …' is repeated four times. This repetition emphasizes the intensely personal nature of the speaker's commitment to the ideals with which he has associated himself. Other words that are repeated are the powerful abstract nouns 'domination' and 'ideal', and the verb 'fought'.

The persuasive nature of the speech is also heightened by the use of balanced and parallel sentence patterns. For example, the sentence 'It is an ideal which I hope to live for and to achieve' balances the two verbs 'live for' and 'achieve' in a parallel structure. The last sentence repeats the structure 'It is an ideal …' and introduces a third possibility that is balanced against the previous two: '… for which I am prepared to die'. This pattern places emphasis on the last idea and in so doing echoes and emphasizes the speaker's unswerving dedication and conviction.

The speech seems to be aimed at a general audience, in spite of the fact that it was delivered during court proceedings. This suggests the speaker's awareness of the fact that it would reach a much wider audience than the immediate one, and also that it would have lasting impact.

First of all, the subject-matter seems to suggest a general adult audience. The subject is about the struggle of the African people, which is a concept that would be accessible to adults from all walks of life. The presentation of abstract concepts suggests that this speech was directed mainly at adults.

The intended audience is also suggested by the sentence patterns. The sentences in the speech are either simple structures or else the main verb is presented first. This type of writing is easier to follow than writing that uses many complex structures where the subordinate clauses come first. This also suggests that the speech may have been intended for a general audience.

The first sentence is an example of a simple structure, with one verb, namely 'have dedicated'. The second sentence is a balanced compound structure, in which the clause 'I have fought ...' is repeated after the conjunction 'and'.

Vocabulary is another indicator of the audience for whom the speech was intended. The vocabulary is not simple, and there are several examples of abstract terms such as 'dedicated', 'cherished' and 'harmony'. This may seem to suggest an educated audience. On the other hand, the vocabulary is not specialized at all. Certain terms are relatively simple and generally accessible, such as 'struggle', 'fought', 'ideal', 'free', and 'equal'. This suggests that the speech is able to reach a wide audience composed of people with different levels of education and social power.

Finally, the tone of the speech is in keeping with its persuasive purpose, and is appropriate both to its subject-matter and to its intended audience. The tone is serious, suggested by words with negative connotations, such as 'struggle' and 'domination'. The tone is also elevated, suggested by the words with positive connotations used to express the speaker's ideals, such as 'democratic', 'ideal', 'free', and 'harmony'.

We hope that this example of discourse analysis has served to demonstrate how you go about such an exercise. Our approach is not the only one, and we may have left out things you would have included, but trust that the exercise helped you to apply our guidelines.

As a second example, we are now going to analyse a very different text.

Example 2

Tomatoes contain plentiful amounts of Vitamin C and carotenoids which, with vitamin A, are known as 'antioxidant' nutrients. These play a vital role in neutralizing unstable molecules known as 'free radicals', produced in the body as a by-product of the oxidation of food to release energy, which can attack and damage body cells.

Speaker/Writer	Context	Audience	Purpose
There is hardly any sense of a particular speaker or writer in this text. The tone is very impersonal and factual. The writer is educated and well-informed about the subject.	This text could have come from a 'live' lecture situation or, if written, a text-book or journal article related to biology, health and the medical field.	Definitely not the general public, but people with more than a superficial interest in diet and health. Possibly nurses, dieticians or medical students. The schemata of such audiences would be likely to make this text coherent.	To *inform*. The speaker or writer is imparting specialist knowledge to a specialist audience. The whole tone of the discourse is academic and educational.

Now to flesh this out into a full analysis:

Speaker/Writer

The impersonal nature of this discourse means that the personality of the writer or speaker does not come across at all. It is impossible to tell what this person's attitudes and values might be. However, it is clear that he or she has specialized knowledge. The speaker/writer uses technical terminology and fairly formal, standard English, revealing that he or she has an academic background.

Context

The speaker/writer assumes a common academic context with the audience. If this is a 'live' interaction, the context is probably a lecture room, or possibly some other professional setting where the speaker is delivering a research topic. If the discourse is written, the source is probably a textbook or other academic text.

Audience

The text is factual and the speaker/writer is giving scientific information on a particular subject. Sentence structures are long and complex, and difficult vocabulary is used. These considerations, together with the fairly technical/scientific language, all suggest that the audience can understand complex sentence structures; would be familiar with this field and these terms; and has the necessary background knowledge, academic training, and schemata to make this discussion coherent.

Purpose

The text is factual and the writer is giving scientific information on a particular subject. The language is formal, precise, and related to a field of academic study. Therefore, the purpose of this text is definitely to *inform*, and has an educational goal.

Again, our next example is very different from the previous example, and thus requires quite different analysis:

Example 3

R250 000

Lovely north-facing family home. Cute and cosy with 3 spacious bedr, 2 bathr. Tropical garden. Excellent security. Close to schools. Neat as a pin.

SNAP IT UP!
Estelle Brown: 082 345987

Speaker/Writer	Context	Audience	Purpose
Estate agent. Personal qualities do not really come through – she is using a 'professional' voice. Nevertheless,	Newspaper advertisement for a house. Language abbreviated for conciseness: newspaper	Middle-class people (judging by the price); heads of families who are seeking a home. They would have children and need to	To *sell* this house. To *persuade* audience that this house is worth viewing and buying (emotive language

the tone is friendly and inviting. Agent adopts a fairly informal register to sound welcoming and approachable to potential buyers.	advertisements are expensive (you pay per character or per word).	feel safe and be near schools. They would be security conscious.	is used to evoke positive emotions). To *inform*: basic facts about house are given.

This framework fleshed out:

Speaker/Writer

The estate agent who placed this advertisement is acting in her professional role. She is obviously motivated to make a sale, so adopts a friendly, positive tone. This may, or may not, be her true personality.

Context

This advertisement probably appears in the classified section of a newspaper. The cost of such advertisements makes brevity essential, so the text is worded as economically as possible with abbreviations: 'bathr'; and omission of verbs and articles: '[It has a] tropical garden'.

Audience

The general public has access to such advertisements, but only those people with families looking for a suitable home would read such texts with attention. We could narrow the market for such a home to middle-income couples planning to have children, or families with children of school-going age.

Purpose

The prime purpose here is to *sell* the house and for no less than the price advertised, if possible. In order to *persuade* readers that the house is worth going to look at, the agent uses emotive language: 'lovely', 'cute', 'cosy', 'neat'. She also tries to create a sense of urgency in the exhortation to 'SNAP IT UP!'

In addition to being persuasive, the agent has to provide some information about the product, so the other purpose is to *inform*. This necessitates the provision of selected facts, such as the price of the house and its specifications, for example the number of bedrooms.

The mixed purpose of persuading and informing creates a style that is both emotive and to some degree factual. The tone, however, is enthusiastic and positive throughout.

In order to practise what you have learned about discourse analysis, answer the following questions on the text below:

Activity 5 Discourse analysis

Study the text below. What does the use of language suggest about:

1 The *producer* (writer or speaker) of the piece?
2 The *context* in which this language was used?
3 The *audience* of this item?
4 The *purpose* for which it was written?

Comment on any other features of the text you think are significant.

> You will need a large chicken for this dish. Cut the chicken into pieces and season well with spices. Place seasoned pieces in a flat, oven-proof dish; cover and bake for one hour at 180 °C. Remove from oven and add sauce, making sure that all pieces are covered. Return to the oven and bake for a further 30 minutes.

Activity 6 Discourse analysis

Study the text below. What does the use of language suggest about:
1 The *producer* (writer or speaker) of the piece?
2 The *context* in which this language was used?
3 The *audience* of this item?
4 The *purpose* for which it was written?

Comment on any other features of the text you think are significant.

Drakensberg four-day breakaway

COME WITH US *as if on the wings of an eagle –*
experience the incredible beauty of the Drakensberg
with its cliffs and valleys. Listen to the echoes of
Golden Gate. Experience the beauty of Champagne
Castle. Fill your soul with the soothing music of the
Drakensberg Boys Choir. Experience God's own
creation. Take part in sports, walks,
horse riding, bowls, golf, etc.

CONTACT US FOR A COLOUR BROCHURE.

Splendour Tours: Tel/Fax (012) 803 9360.

Activity 7 Discourse analysis

Study the text below. What does the use of language suggest about:

1 The *producer* (writer or speaker) of the piece?
2 The *context* in which this language was used?
3 The *audience* of this item?
4 The *purpose* for which it was written?

Comment on any other features of the text you think are significant.

Students inconsiderate

IT IS COMMON PRACTICE that there are students bent on destroying the future of others in the Republic of South Africa, especially in Pretoria.

I am a student at Unisa and in my third year towards a five-year degree. This year I decided to become a member of the Sammy Marks Library. But the same problem that I experienced at Unisa is also prevalent here at Sammy Marks library – disturbance.

As I write this letter in the library, a tall and well-built man (I'm afraid of fighting because I was born very thin), is discussing events of the past weekend with his friend, and there is no security in sight to call him to order. What a shame!

Students are often so arrogant that they come and sit on the edge of a desk and discuss whatever nonsense they want to talk about with others while another student who is trying to study is sitting right next to them. I don't think retaliation is the best remedy.

So, I urge the management of the Sammy Marks Library to take drastic steps against those arrogant students who deliberately want to stand between the bright future of hardworking students and their studies.

Student, Atteridgeville

Pretoria News, 7 February, 2002

SUMMARY

The most important points dealt with in this final chapter are listed below:

- The meaning of the terms: 'discourse' and 'text analysis'.
- A suggested approach to discourse analysis.
- The effect on discourse of the speaker/writer, context, audience and purpose.
- The effect of the above factors on the style and tone of the discourse.

GLOSSARY

Here is a list of some important terms used in this chapter. Fill in the missing definitions, and add other terms and definitions.

discourse
_____
_____

text
_____
_____

discourse analysis
_____
_____

tone
_____
_____

style
_____
_____

ENDNOTES

1   This strategy for discourse analysis is adapted from *Your own words* (Chapter 5), by Judith Wainwright and Jackie Hutton. 1992. Walton-on-Thames: Nelson.

2   NELSON MANDELA. 1994. *Long walk to freedom*, p. 322. Boston: Little, Brown.

Conclusion

We have dealt with a number of diverse language-related issues in this book. Many have been purely linguistic in nature; for example, the functions that language performs in our lives, and how language is related to thought – issues that are universal. We have discussed the power of language to create and change perceptions, to hurt and offend, or to encourage and uplift others. We have also looked at the 'nuts' and 'bolts' of language: words; sentences and longer 'chunks' of language (or discourse) and suggested some practical strategies for analysing these.

Other issues we have dealt with relate to the extraordinarily complex language situation we have in South Africa specifically, with its eleven official languages. The fact that English is the only world language in the South African context gives it a special importance but also creates problems, some of which we have touched on. We have considered what constitutes 'standard' English, and why it is considered desirable to become proficient in the standard variety. We hope we have drawn you into the lively debate about the role and status of English – and particularly standard English – in South Africa.

We have attempted to promote an awareness of the rich linguistic variety in our young democracy, as well as of the challenges it gives rise to. The fundamental aim underlying all our discussion has been to foster tolerance for the diversity of languages and language varieties in South Africa.

Language is a hugely important tool for understanding ourselves and our society, and for resolving conflict. It can function both as a barrier and as a channel of communication between people. We need to understand the complex forces that have shaped and continue to shape language, by studying and analysing language and language issues in an objective way. Such an approach is a way of overcoming the kind of prejudice and negative perceptions that can exist among groups of people who speak English in a variety of ways. Language study can thus help to bring about awareness, perspective, and mutual respect.

We hope that, by providing and discussing information about language, we have enabled you to participate knowledgeably in activities and debates involving language in a way that will further the ideals of respect and tolerance.

Felicity Horne and Glenda Heinemann

Suggested answers to the activities in this book

CHAPTER 1

Activity 1 The spread of English

1 Political and military power (such as that enjoyed by Britain during the period of the British Empire) contributes to the spread of the language spoken by those who wield that power.

Economic power has the same influence, in this case, trade links established by Britain during the time of Empire. The rise of the United States, which conducts business in English and has a powerful role in world markets, has further contributed to the spread of the English language.

Religious influence does not seem to have been a major factor in the spread of English internationally. Religious influence contributed to the spread of Latin in western Europe during the Middle Ages.

Computer technology and the electronic media have expanded the use of English in the modern world enormously and they continue to do so.

2 The speakers of a world language would enjoy a great advantage over speakers of other languages, in terms of their influence in world affairs and scientific research.

3 The power and influence of the English language could be seen to *exclude* those who have not mastered it. There is also the danger that proficiency in languages other than English may be sacrificed.

4 Although English is only one of eleven official languages in South Africa, it is the language of Parliament and, to a large extent, of politics; it is the language of business and tertiary education, and the language that gives access to the wider world. People who speak English are at an advantage.

5 As a language comes to be used by people from all over the world, these new speakers would use the English language to express their own identity, and could develop forms of the language that may not be understood by other speakers of the same language in other places. This could lead to loss of *mutual intelligibility* among speakers of such varieties of English.

Activity 2 The value of primary language and culture

1 The writer regards it as tragic when children lose their primary language, since this means breaking ties with family, community, cultural, and historical roots. He strongly disapproves of parents who allow or encourage this to happen to their children.

2 Own opinion, informed by an understanding that losing a primary language usually entails losing cultural values, traditions, identity, community, and family cohesion.

3 Such parents obviously want their children to have access to higher education and certain job opportunities. These parents seem to prize these things more than maintaining the family traditions and culture of the primary language.

4 Of course, being able to speak English fluently is not synonymous with being clever. Highly intelligent individuals may not be proficient in English. Language proficiency depends on numerous factors, of which intelligence is only one.

Furthermore, it is not possible to speak any language 'without an accent'. We all have accents of one kind or another. What the writer probably means is that the child can speak English without a Zulu accent.

5 When a child is 'culturally alienated', this means that he or she is estranged or separated from the cultural group he or she was born into. Cultural alienation removes the sense of belonging to that particular community and culture.

6 Own opinion, but again, this should be backed up with sound reasons. As far as whose responsibility it is to maintain the mother tongue, parents should surely bear the prime responsibility, since the primary language is acquired in the pre-school years and in the home. The role of the school only occurs later. Ideally, the school should build on the language foundation laid in the family environment. The father's attitude of blame towards the school seems unreasonable and irresponsible.

7 It is possible to reach some sort of compromise on this question. Children can learn an additional language, such as English, at school, as well as maintain their primary tongue. Such a system is known as *additive bilingualism*. The case of the Zulu child in this passage is an example of the *subtractive* approach to additional-language teaching: the child loses a language instead of gaining one. The South African education policy follows the additive model.

Activity 3 Comparison of editorials

Editorial 1: **Time to turn talk into action**	Editorial 2: **Another English Invasion**
English marginalizes, dominates and will destroy other languages.	Other languages are not threatened by English and will survive.
English is forcefully imposed on everyone.	The dominance of the English language has occurred naturally through technological advancement.
Children are disadvantaged by being forced to learn through the medium of English.	(Implied) Everyone will need English so it is to the advantage of all children to master it.
The supremacy of the English language is discriminatory, unjust, and goes against the South African Constitution.	The dominance of English is a practical reality so learning it is an essential survival skill.
We must resist the dominance of the English language.	We must accept the dominance of the English language.

CHAPTER 2

Activity 1 Poetry and dialect

1   'Da same, da same' by Sipho Sepamla is written in a South African dialect, which is mostly English but includes some Afrikaans influences. The word 'clearlink' is an unusual English translation of the Afrikaans word 'kleurling' ('coloured'), and 'Africa' is spelled the Afrikaans way ('Afrika'). Mixing English and Afrikaans is a major feature of the so-called Cape Coloured dialect.

   The use of grammar in the poem is irregular. There is lack of concord or subject/verb agreement ('I doesn't'); an absence of verbs ('you black' instead of 'you are black'), and a non-standard tense of verbs ('He make' instead of 'He made'). There is an absence of a noun, and a repeated use of an adjective in its place ('you gotta big terrible, *terrible* ...'); there is phonetic spelling of non-standard pronunciations (the use of 'of' instead of 'if' in 'I doesn't care of you black'; 'avarybudy' for 'everybody'; 'diflent' for 'different'; 'Saus' for 'South'; 'da' for 'the', 'anader' for 'another'); and grammatically clumsy, non-standard expressions ('dat's for meaning to say').

   Whether you describe these examples as 'errors' or 'non-standard features' would depend on the stance you took: either prescriptive or descriptive.

2   No. This poem would be less easily understood by non-South Africans. In the first place, they would probably not know the language of Afrikaans, and so would not understand the words borrowed from Afrikaans. They would not know the Cape Coloured dialect and accent, so would be confused by the phonetic spelling of words like 'saus'.

3   Standard English version of the first stanza:
   I don't care if you're black
   I don't care if you're white
   I don't care if you're Indian
   I don't care if you're coloured
   But sometimes you South Africans
   Have a big and terrible problem
   Somewhere inside yourselves.

   You probably found that you had to do a bit of guesswork as to what exactly you thought the poet wanted to say in some instances. Even though you may have understood the gist of the poem well, you may not have been too sure of your accuracy in rewording it. For example, the second 'terrible' in line 6 is translated as 'problem', but it could also be 'pain', 'blindness', 'attitude', 'prejudice' or even 'evil'. It is also not possible to be absolutely sure of what 'sometimes' in line 5 means so it has been left as is in the version above.

4   Whether the poem is more effective in the original dialect or in standard English is a matter of opinion. However, the distinctive speech style (converted into the written form) adds interest and would be more likely to attract and hold the attention of the reader.

The poet's chosen style of expression is surely deliberate: he must be aiming at a particular effect. He could be trying to show that although the speaker is uneducated, he has insight into the abnormality of his society, dominated as it is by racial prejudices. Everyone's perceptions are distorted, and as people so often see one another as less than human, everyone is diminished and everyone suffers loss of humanity.

Unsophisticated as this speaker appears to be (if one were to judge him by his command of 'standard' English), he expresses profound truths. It is indeed true that our blood is the same colour beneath our skin and that we all have the same feelings. Through the sharp contrast between the wisdom of the speaker's observations and the simplicity of his style of speech, he conveys the point that a man with a limited education and language proficiency can nevertheless be clear-sighted in his vision, and more humane, than those who may consider themselves his 'superior'.

Many people taking a prescriptive stance may dismiss the speaker's point of view because he would be regarded as simple and ignorant, but the point he makes is no less moving than the words spoken by Shakespeare's Shylock in *The Merchant of Venice*:

'I am a Jew. Hath not a Jew eyes? hath not a Jew hands, organs, dimensions, senses, affections, passions? ... If you prick us, do we not bleed?'

(III, i, 55–61)

Activity 2   Viewpoint underlying letter to the editor

The writer of this letter is definitely operating from a *prescriptive* position. He or she is highly critical of the pronunciation of English additional-language speakers. The word 'cure' in: 'Will it not be a cure if ... we shut down the TV

...' is very revealing: it suggests that non-standard features are a form of language disease! The words 'should be' and 'correctly' in: 'it should be spoken clearly and correctly' are strongly prescriptive in tone.

(An ironic aside: although the writer of this letter assumes the position of a language 'expert', he or she uses the word 'shibboleth' very strangely, leaving one in some doubt as to whether he or she understands the meaning of the word. You may like to look this word up in the dictionary yourself.)

Activity 3 Prescriptive viewpoint of a newspaper column

Robert Kirby's examples of objectionable language usage:

- *'The petrol price has gone up **with** 60 cents ...'*

Corrected version:
*'The petrol price has gone up **by** 60 cents ...'*

- *'If it **will reach** the R3 mark ...'*

Corrected version:
*'If it **reaches** the R3 mark ...'*

- *'One of eight people **are** being charged ...'*

Corrected version:
*'One of eight people **is** being charged ...'*

- *'... fourfeeted ...'*

Corrected version:
'... forfeited ...' (Stress on first syllable; second syllable pronounced *'fit'*)

- *'...confisticated...'*

Corrected version:
'...confiscated ...' (extra syllable dropped)

- *'The persons found in **the** possession of the drugs ...'*

Corrected version:
'The persons found **in possession** of the drugs ...'

- '... can be full prosecuted...'

Corrected version:
'... **will** be prosecuted...'

Activity 4 Applying prescriptive and descriptive approaches

1 Commentary on poem from a *prescriptive* point of view:
   In order to have demonstrated an understanding of the prescriptive approach, you would have been disapproving and critical regarding the use of language in this poem. You would have rejected the poet's deviations from standard English, which, you would have implied, is the only correct model:

   In this poem the speaker makes serious grammatical mistakes. The language is mixed and shows gross ignorance of how English should be spoken. All in all, the rules of grammar are broken. The use of language is incorrect and therefore unacceptable.

2 Commentary on poem from a *descriptive* point of view:
   In order to have demonstrated this point of view you would have described the language of the poem as objectively as possible. You would have drawn attention to and described its non-standard features, but without a disapproving attitude:

   The dialect used in this poem is South African in origin and is spoken by some people chiefly in the Western Cape region of the country. Its non-standard features include the mixing of languages (English and Afrikaans), lack of subject/verb agreement, and phonetic spelling. This non-standard variety of English is highly expressive and colourful.

   If you compare these two rather brief commentaries, you will notice that they both point out some of the same features of the passage, but the tone, emphasis, and conclusions of the comments are very different. The prescriptive commentary is judgemental, whereas the descriptive one seeks to examine and understand the language usage in the poem.

Activity 5 Non-standard English in the classroom

When thinking about this question, you needed to be sensitive to the fact that denigrating the non-standard features of a child's dialect is likely to cause distressing emotional conflict in the child and could possibly alienate him or her from his or her family and cultural roots. The child's dialect should be shown acceptance by the teacher.

However, it is necessary to teach standard English as an additional, alternative variety to be used when appropriate. The child will need to be taught, for example, that one does not mix languages in certain situations, and that subject and verb should agree ('*I do*', not '*I does*').

The teacher could demonstrate and create awareness that different situations call for different kinds of language use. The child needs to know and needs to be able to use the standard variety for some important applications. When writing public examinations or business letters, or speaking in oral examinations or interviews, for example, the individual would need to have a command of the standard variety of the language. Not knowing the basic grammatical rules of the standard variety of English would place the child at a serious disadvantage in the wider world beyond the home.

CHAPTER 3

Activity 1 Text-mapping

Your mind-map showing the different functions of language could have taken different forms, but a simple one would show the main topic ('The Functions of Language') in a circle in the centre of the page. From this central circle lines would branch outwards, showing each of the functions of language (shown as subheadings in this chapter), and also enclosed in circles.

If you wanted to make your mind-map more detailed, you could add points relating to each of these functions, connecting them to the relevant functions with lines. You could enclose these points inside a square or oblong to differentiate them from the central idea and each of the language functions. Alternatively, you could use colour to differentiate the different levels, such as red for the main idea; green for the functions; and purple for the points relating to the functions.

Remember that a mind-map is a way of *summarizing* and *organizing* information so as to clarify understanding and to help memorize information.

Cluttered mind-maps are not helpful. Avoid clutter by using only key words and short phrases, not whole sentences, and omit minor details and examples.

Here is our example: yours may look rather different from ours but may be just as helpful.

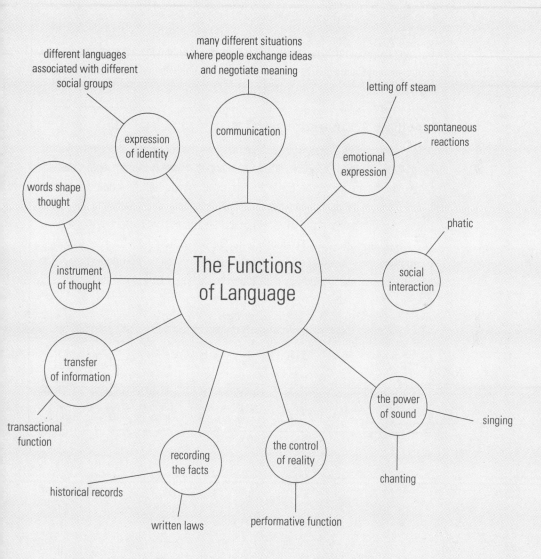

Activity 2 The relationship between language and thought: your own experience

Obviously your answers would be individual, but we hope that the question provoked some self-reflection about your own habits regarding the use of language as an aid to thought and memory. Do you write down things you have to do in the coming day, or week? Do you write out a shopping list before you go to the shops? Do you make silent 'mental notes' to help you remember things? If so, you are using language to help you think.

But there are probably other times when you allow your thoughts to wander in an unstructured, random way. This type of thought does not seem to depend on language, unless you choose to tell someone else what you are thinking about.

Activity 3 Categorization

To complete this activity, you would first need to recognize that all the words are types of food. *Food* would be your *superordinate* term, or main heading. You could categorize the foods further by arranging the individual foods into *food groups*, using subheadings to do so. Under each of these subheadings you would need to divide the words so that they fall into the correct category.

You may have chosen slightly different words from ours for your subheadings ('starches', perhaps, instead of 'grains' to include porridge, bread, and cereals), but your general organization should have been much the same.

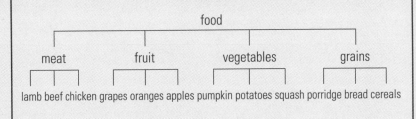

CHAPTER 4

Activity 1 The use of official languages in South Africa

We hope that you filled in the table with as many examples as you could find. Please go on collecting examples as you study and become aware of the uses of language that you encounter.

Activity 2 Summary of extracts from articles

Summary **1** was a summary of the extract from the article by **Titlestad**.

Summary **2** = **Ndebele**

Summary **3** = **McArthur**

Summary **4** = **Mphahlele**

Summary **5** = **Butler**

Activity 3 Language change

Author 1	Author 2	Author 3	Author 4	Author 5
Ndebele	**Mphahlele**	**McArthur**	**Butler**	**Titlestad**

(If you have placed McArthur as author 4 and Butler as author 3, this would be quite acceptable.)

Activity 4

The value of this exercise lay in expressing and organizing your own ideas. There can be no single 'correct' answer here.

CHAPTER 5

Activity 1 Your own identity

We hope you gave this exercise a good deal of thought. There are obviously no right or wrong answers here!

Activity 2 Your own idiolect

Here, too, we cannot comment on your answers, but we hope you have observed as many aspects of your spoken language as possible, especially your choice of words and expressions.

Activity 3 South African dialects

1 'Just now' can refer to past or future. It is also very vague because it does not indicate how long ago in the past, or when in the future. In Britain the phrase is much more specific and refers only to the immediate present: 'at the moment', or the recent past.

2 Descriptive.

3 We know that the writer is taking a *descriptive approach* towards this South African dialect because he obviously delights in the colour and humour of South African English as we see in words like 'enriched' and in the final statement 'Where would our conversation be without them?' He gives examples and comments without suggesting disapproval.

   If he were being prescriptive, he would be judging the language according to the rules of 'correct' standard English and condemning the language because it deviates from this 'norm'.

4 *We are going to **Johannesburg soon/shortly**.*
   ***Are you**?*
   Yes**! Do you want to come **with us?

Activity 4 'Yeah mtshana...'

1 **Syntax**   This text is still recognizable as a form of English because the basic sentence structures (syntax) are mostly those used in English. However, there are some non-standard grammatical features; for example, some unusual constructions, and some adjectives are used as nouns: ('die *clevers*').

There is also a great deal of use of the apostrophe (addressing an imaginary person): '*Yeah, mtshana*'; *Ja, Jack*'.

Lexis   These include the incorporation of Afrikaans words and those of other indigenous languages. Certain words are clipped in a colloquial way: *'bros'* for brothers. Slang usage abounds: *'cherries'* for girls, and *'laaities'* for youngsters.

Phonology   Phonetic spelling indicates pronunciation: *'mtshana'* for 'my china' (colloquialism for 'my friend', originating, as a matter of interest, in the Cockney rhyming slang 'my china plate' meaning 'my mate').

This dialect appears to be a version of the post-colonial, post-apartheid South African English slang *Iscamtho*, mixing together languages from South Africa: Nguni languages, English, and Afrikaans. The writer creates the 'in-group' feeling by using colloquial words and phrases from several languages, and also by using a familiar manner to address the audience.

2   Non-South Africans would find this dialect very difficult, if not impossible, to follow. They would not be able to understand much of the content of the text because the lexis consists largely of indigenous languages. This dialect is only likely to be fully intelligible among the 'in-group' of *Iscamtho* speakers.

3   In terms of basic communication, this text illustrates the sheer practical advantages of using the standard variety of a language. The standard form enables intelligibility, while the dialect forms do not, except to speakers of the dialect.

CHAPTER 6

Activity 1 Differences between speech and writing

Here is the completed table:

Speech	Writing
Substance The substance is phonic (sound caused by air-pressure movements in the vocal tract).	**Substance** The substance is graphic (visual marks on a surface).
Time Speech is usually time-bound and transient (impermanent).	**Time** Writing is permanent.
Space Both participants are present.	**Space** Writing is space-bound (the writer is distant from the recipient).
Planning With the exception of prepared speeches, spoken language is usually spontaneous and not planned in advance.	**Planning** Writing can be organized and planned in advance.
Division into units Speech relies on intonation and pauses to 'divide utterances into manageable chunks'.	**Division into units** Division can be indicated by means of layout, design, and punctuation.
Context Meaning is often indicated by context or situation; participants can make use of expressions such as *this one*, *over there* to convey meaning.	**Context** As participants cannot see one another, they cannot rely on the context to make meaning clear.

Contrasts

Some contrasts cannot be conveyed in speech, but changes in volume and pitch of the voice can draw attention to contrasts.

Contrasts

Contrasts can be indicated by means of punctuation and capitalization, for example.

Grammar and lexis

Colloquial words and expressions are commonly used and regarded as acceptable. Sentences are often incomplete and change as the conversation goes along. Many non-standard features may be present.

Grammar and lexis

Grammatical constructions are complete in writing; some technical words are used in writing but seldom in speech.

Formality

Speech tends to be less formal than writing.

Formality

Written language tends to be more formal than speech.

Special uses

Spoken language is used less often than writing for special purposes. However, special forms of spoken language are set aside for ceremonial or religious purposes.

Special uses

Written language sometimes has special status in legal and religious contexts.

Activity 2 Your own speech and writing

Your answers will have been individual, but you probably use speech most often for daily interaction. This speech is mostly spontaneous and informal. In some contexts speech is essential and writing inappropriate (as in the case of communicating with pre-school children). Writing may be too slow (if, for example, a sudden emergency requires an urgent warning). However, there are circumstances in which you will definitely have to use written language. These would include writing out a shopping list before leaving for the supermarket, and writing notes when you study academic texts. In your working life there are many specific tasks that require you to use written language. Both kinds of language – speech and writing – serve important purposes for different applications.

Activity 3   What makes a conversation successful

Your mind-map will have been your individual way of summarizing the 'rules' governing successful conversations.

Activity 4   Conversational turns and exchanges

1   English conversation and analysis

We hope you have done an analysis of a real conversation. It is not possible to comment here, as each one will be unique.

2   Conversations in languages other than English

Here, too, we hope you took the trouble to think about the 'rules' for conversation in the other languages you know. For example, did you consider whether silence is regarded as rude, or as acceptable? What about interrupting someone while they are speaking? Or waiting to be addressed before you speak? Are two people allowed to speak at the same time?

Activity 5   Your description of a good conversationalist

1   Your description will obviously have been individual, but we hope it was informed by the discussion and explanations in this chapter, as well as by your own personal observations.

2   Your answer should be based on what you have read and thought about in this chapter, as well as on your knowledge of the languages you speak.

Activity 6   Implicatures

1   **A**: *What's the time?*
    B: *The news is over.*
    When A asks about the time, B assumes or infers that A wants to listen to the news on the television or radio. This is the first implicature. B then establishes the time; realizes it is too late for the news; and relates the fact that the news is over to A. A has to infer that it is later than he or she thought and so has missed the news.
      Of course some implicatures can be wrong and lead to misunderstanding. Perhaps A wants to know the time for some reason other than listening to the news. B's response would then be irrelevant and unhelpful.

2   **A**: *Was that thunder I heard?*
    B: *I must close the windows.*
    A: *I'm sorry, I'm busy.*

When A remarks on the thunder, B infers that rain is imminent – the first implicature. B knows that the windows of the house are open and if it rains, water will get in. B does not state these things but assumes that they will be understood, so these are also implicatures. B states that he or she must close the windows, assuming perhaps that A will help him or her to do this. Whether or not this assumption is intended, A infers that he or she is expected to help close the windows. A is busy, and informs B of this, but does not state the final implicature in this little exchange: that because A is busy, he or she will not be able to help A close the windows. A implies that he or she cannot comply with B's unstated (and perhaps unintended) request for help.

3   In the first frame, the doctor tells Hagar that he is too tense and must try to eliminate stress from his life. In the second frame, Hagar 'reports' this advice to Helga, his wife, by saying that her mother cannot visit them anymore.

What Hagar reports to his wife bears no resemblance to the doctor's words at all. We, the readers, have to fill in the gaps or guess the implicature(s), unstated by Hagar, that link the two scenes of the comic strip. These implicatures correspond to Hagar's thought processes, which go something like this:

I must eliminate stress from my life. → *What causes me stress?* → *My mother-in-law.* → *She irritates me.* → *I don't want to see her again.* → *I will tell Helga she cannot visit us any more.*

It appears that to Hagar, there is a clear, logical line of reasoning here, so that he feels it is quite legitimate to tell Helga that the doctor said her mother can no longer visit them. He tells her this as though he is reporting the exact words the doctor uttered, but of course he is not. His statement to Helga is the conclusion he has reached after *a series of unstated inferences* or implicatures he has drawn from the doctor's words.

(For those of you who do not follow the Hagar cartoons, Hagar is a Viking who is regularly involved in battle. The joke is that he appears to regard a visit from his mother-in-law as much more stressful than the dangers of hand-to-hand combat. It could be that because he obviously does not like his mother-in-law, he chooses to name her as his chief source of stress – a convenient label! This is very typical of the way we human beings manipulate information and use language to suit ourselves.)

CHAPTER 7

Activity 1 Abusive terms

'Hurtful and abusive' terms such as '*meid*' and '*boer*' are not intrinsically offensive (or were not at one time), but have become so through usage and the change of contexts. The word '*boer*', for example, has the simple, denotative meaning of 'farmer' in Afrikaans, but over time has acquired associations of a particular 'White' ethnic group associated with the Afrikaans language and right-wing, anti-'Black' attitudes. It has now become strongly pejorative, but in certain contexts only. If used as a term of ethnic abuse, it is out of order, but presumably it can still be used in a legitimate way to denote its original, literal meaning.

The word 'meid' (meaning 'maid' or 'domestic servant', which was often applied to all black African females regardless of occupation) came to suggest the way African females were perceived: in perpetual servitude. The role of servant, thus, was the paramount 'characteristic', obliterating individual human qualities. The fact that new laws have been passed to forbid the use of such terms shows recognition of the power of language to reflect and spread such negative perceptions.

The terms 'boer' and 'meid' are examples of *racist stereotyping*.

Activity 2 Taboos and euphemisms

We hope you were able to think of some additional euphemisms of your own to add to the examples provided in the table.

Activity 3 Job advertisement

The euphemism in this advertisement lies in the phrase: '(AA ONLY)'. This of course means 'Affirmative Action Only', and is an indirect way of saying that only 'previously disadvantaged people' (a circumlocution denoting black African people) need apply. The advertiser has to word this carefully, because if he were to say straight out: 'Only blacks wanted', he would be guilty of racial discrimination in terms of the Constitution, so he uses a euphemistic 'code' ('AA') to indicate preferred race.

Activity 4 Place names

Completed table:

Old	New
Hendrik Verwoerd Dam	Gariep Dam
Jan Smuts Airport	Johannesburg International Airport
Rhodesia	Zimbabwe
South West Africa	Namibia
Lourenço Marques	Maputo
John Vorster Square	Johannesburg Central Police Station
Pietersburg	Polokwane
Voortrekkerhoogte	Thaba Tshwane

Activity 5 Place names: attitudes

Name of person concerned	Positive or negative attitude towards the name change
1 Jan Kriel	Negative
2 Raymond Mashilo Kgagudi and Jacob Wistebaar	Positive
3 Terence Beard	Negative
4 Johan Viljoen	Negative

CHAPTER 8

Activity 1 Context and meaning

1 (a) *intelligence*
In the first sentence 'intelligence' means *cleverness*, or *intellectual ability*. In the second sentence 'intelligence' means *information*.

(b) *measures*
In the first sentence, 'measures' means a *unit of measurement*, such as a cup, or any standard quantity of something.
In the second sentence, 'measures' means *steps*, or *action taken to achieve a purpose*.

2 (a) *patient*
Your sentences will obviously be original, but here are our examples:

The *patient* was transferred to a different hospital for treatment.
A teacher needs to be very *patient* to work with children who have learning problems.

Activity 2 Constituent morphemes

2 *elements* = basic morpheme *element* + suffix *-s* expressing plural form of the noun.
3 *irregular* = basic morpheme *regular* + prefix *ir-* to indicate the negative form of the adjective.
4 *clearer* = basic morpheme *clear* + suffix *-er* to express the comparative form of the adjective.
5 *worthy* = basic morpheme *worth* + suffix *-y* to change the word class from a noun to an adjective.
6 *impossible* = basic morpheme *possible* + prefix *im-* to indicate the negative form of the adjective.
7 *cheapest* = basic morpheme *cheap* + suffix *-est* to express the superlative form of the adjective.
8 *uninteresting* = basic morpheme *interest* + suffix *–ing* to change the word class from a noun to an adjective, as well as the prefix *un-* to indicate negative.

Activity 3 Word-formation processes

1	*plane*	**Clipping**: shortened form of *aeroplane*
	faction	**Blending**: *fact* and *fiction*
2	*PANSALB*	**Acronym**: **Pan S**outh **A**frican **L**anguage **B**oard
	website	**Compounding**: *web* and *site* as well as **Coining**: new word for new phenomenon
3	*bouquet*	**Borrowing**: French word
4	*Disagreement*	**Derivation**: new word created from adding the prefix *dis-* and the suffix *-ment* to the basic morpheme *agree*
	dorp	**Borrowing**: Afrikaans word
5	*Phone*	**Clipping**: shortened form of *telephone*
	cell	**Clipping**: shortened form of *cellular telephone*
6	*NEPAD*	**Acronym**: **Ne**w **P**artnership for **A**frican **D**evelopment
7	*party*	**Conversion**: word changes its function (from noun to verb) without a change of form
8	*rehab*	**Clipping**: shortened form of *rehabilitation centre*
	inhumane	**Derivation**: prefix *in-* added to basic morpheme *humane* to create negative form of adjective
9	*finger*	**Conversion**: word changes its function (from noun to verb) without a change of form
10	*toyi-toyi*	**Borrowing**: Ndebele and Shona word
	courtroom	**Compounding**: *court* and *room*

Activity 4 Word classes

Your sentences will have been individual, but here are our examples:

mark	The student was awarded a good *mark* for the essay. (Noun)
	I have to *mark* examination papers next week. (Verb)
	Please pass me my *mark* book. (Adjective)
paint	I need to buy more *paint* to complete the outside wall. (Noun)
	The artist was commissioned to *paint* the portrait. (Verb)
	The *paint* box was old and well-used. (Adjective)
bottle	The baby sucked contentedly at his *bottle*. (Noun)
	There was so much fruit, we had to *bottle* the surplus. (Verb)
	Use a *bottle* brush to wash the baby's bottle thoroughly. (Adjective)

Activity 5 Recognizing word classes

1 When lifting the rock, he hurt his *back*. (Noun)
2 Please *back* our efforts to raise money for the school library. (Verb)
3 Give *back* her doll at once. (Adverb)
4 The intruder entered through the *back* door. (Adjective)

Activity 6 Selecting word classes

1 *The poor bear* crouched in the back of the cage.
Here 'poor' is an *adjective* meaning 'pitiful'. It describes the *noun* 'bear', which denotes a large furry mammal.

2 *The poor bear* many hardships because they cannot afford comfort.
'Poor' is usually an adjective describing the quality of not having money or resources. However, in this sentence it functions as a *noun*, standing for 'poor people'. (One of the ways of recognizing a noun is the fact that you can place *a*, *an*, or *the* before it.)

'Bear' functions as a *verb*, meaning 'suffer' or 'endure'.

Once we have recognized the appropriate word classes, the meaning of the sentence becomes clear: 'poor people have to endure difficulties because they lack money to make life comfortable'.

CHAPTER 9

Activity 1 Finding cohesive links

Toloki notices that in every shack they visit, the women are never still. They are always doing something with their hands. They are cooking. They are sewing. They are outside scolding the children. They are at the tap drawing water. They are washing clothes. They are sweeping the floor in their shacks, and the ground outside. They are closing holes in the shacks with cardboard and plastic. They are loudly joking with their neighbours while they hang washing on the line. Or they are fighting with the neighbours about children who have beaten up their own children. They are preparing to go to the taxi rank to catch taxis to the city, where they will work in the kitchen of their madams.

Men, on the other hand, tend to cloud their heads with pettiness and vain pride. They sit all day and dispense wide-ranging philosophies on how things should be. With great authority in their voices, they come up with wise theories on how to put the world right. Then at night they demand to be given food, as if the food just walked into the house on its own. When they believe all the children are asleep, they want to be pleasured. The next day they wake up and continue with their empty theories.

From *Ways of dying* by Zakes Mda

When you are required to point out cohesion in a text, some cohesive features will stand out more than others. What struck us most about this piece was its time-frame, created by the tense of the verbs. So *verb tense* is the first feature we comment on.

Verb tenses

This entire passage is written in the *present tense*. This includes both the *simple present*: 'Toloki notices …', and the *present continuous*: 'They are cooking. They are sewing. They are outside scolding…'

The use of the present tense creates a sense of immediacy and constant activity, which reinforces the point that the women in this community are always very busy. This active mood binds all the separate activities together, creating *cohesion*.

Repeated forms

Repetitive words and sentences are a very obvious feature of this passage. Consider the many: 'They are … they are …' constructions in the first paragraph. There is a series of several short sentences which create a certain repetitive rhythm: 'They are cooking. They are sewing. They are outside scolding the children. They are at the tap drawing water. They are washing clothes …'

Lexical relationships

A great number of words fall into the field of domestic chores: 'cooking', 'sewing', 'washing', 'hanging out clothes', 'scolding children', for example. These are all *actions*.

Another lexical chain concerns the *objects* that would be commonly found in a poor community living in an informal settlement: 'shack', 'tap', 'cardboard', and 'plastic'.

In contrast to the activity of the women who are busily involved with real, down-to-earth practical tasks, another lexical chain in the second paragraph relates to the way the men waste time in *daydreaming* and *idle speculation*: 'cloud their heads', 'pettiness', 'vain pride', 'philosophies', 'theories', and 'empty theories'.

Co-reference

The frequently repeated pronouns 'they' and 'their' refer back to 'women' in the first paragraph, and 'men' in the second. 'Its' in the second paragraph refers back to 'food'.

Conjunctive relations/logical connectors

'Or' and 'where', are logical connectors in the first paragraph. (There are so many short separate sentences in the first paragraph, that very few conjunctions are used.)

Many more conjunctive relations are present in the second paragraph. 'On the other hand', in the first line, signals an important *contrast* in the description of the behaviour of the women and men. 'And', 'then', and 'when' connect the description of observed male behaviour.

(You may have found other cohesive devices we have missed; if you have, well done!)

Activity 2 Sequence of sentences

The logical order of the jumbled sentences in paragraphs 1 and 2 is:

Paragraph 1

Harry Potter was a highly unusual boy in many ways. For one thing, he hated the summer holidays more than any other time of the year. For another, he really wanted to do his homework, but was forced to do it in secret, in the dead of night. And he also happened to be a wizard.

Paragraph 2

In the late summer of that year we lived in a house in a village that looked across the river to the mountains. In the bed of the river there were pebbles and boulders, and the water was clear and blue. Troops went past the house and down the road, and the dust they raised powdered the leaves of the trees. The trunks of the trees were also dusty.

CHAPTER 10

Activity 1 Producer of language (speaker or writer)

1 'So I says to him if he doesn't watch it, I'll donder him stukkend.'
This speaker is probably not a mother-tongue speaker of English, judging by the non-standard use of the verb 'says', and the inclusion of the Afrikaans words 'donder' and 'stukkend'. The informal nature of the language would indicate that it is spoken rather than written. The speaker is probably young and male – if the physical threat is anything to go by – and the personality sounds aggressive.

2 'The exquisite view filled my soul with rapture.'
This speaker/writer sounds educated, with a literary background, and expresses himself or herself in standard English. He or she is responsive to beauty and is poetic by nature.

3 'My father she is very sick.'
This speaker is not a mother-tongue speaker of English, as we can tell from the non-standard use of the pronoun 'she', which is both unnecessary and does not agree with the gender of the word father. This particular deviation from standard English is typical of speakers of the Nguni languages.

4 'The economic indicators on the stock exchange show that the rand is strengthening in relation to other world currencies.'
This speaker is educated, with mother-tongue proficiency in English, and appears to have specialist knowledge in the field of economics and marketing. The specialist terminology is used skilfully, and in a way that suggests the speaker is very used to it.

5 'Wow! What a great movie!'
This speaker sounds young, since he or she uses colloquialisms ('Wow!' and 'great') that are not often used by an older generation. The personality that comes through is that of a spontaneous, lively individual who expresses emotional reactions freely.

Activity 2 Context

1 'Avaunt! and quit my sight! Let the earth hide thee!
Thy bones are marrowless, thy blood is cold;
Thou hast no speculation in those eyes,
Which thou dost glare with.'

Archaic words such as 'Avaunt', 'thee', 'thy' and 'thou', indicate that this text is not contemporary but comes from an earlier historical period. In fact, it comes from Shakespeare's *Macbeth* (III, iv, 93–6) as some of you may have recognized. The words are spoken in reaction to the sight of a ghost, and so are very dramatic, and in keeping with a Jacobean Gothic tragedy.

2 'Viva! Viva! Freedom to all! Amandla!'

These words are associated with the context of a political protest meeting or rally at which feelings are being stirred up against something which is perceived to be restrictive. The word 'Amandla' comes from the Nguni language group and has associations with the freedom struggle in South Africa.

3 'How do you plead? Guilty, or not guilty?'

These words imply the context of a court of law, in which the accused is being asked to plead before the hearing of a case against him or her. The questions are legal convention in such situations.

4 'Come on, ladies and gentlemen, put your hands together for the singing sensation of the decade!'

Here the context is some form of concert or show at which performers are appearing and speaking before a live audience.

Activity 3 Audience

1 'Sit down and stop talking at once, unless you want to stay in at break!'

This audience would be a class of schoolchildren. They are being spoken 'down' to by a figure of authority who feels he or she must exercise power over them.

2 'Pamper yourself with the lingering perfume of creamy *Rosefair* body lotion.

The intended audience seems to be female, and wealthy enough to afford luxuries. The audience would further consist of those women who are beauty-conscious.

3 'In this semester you will learn about different mutations of this specific virus.'

The audience would seem to be a group of medical students listening to a lecture.

4 'Go bundu-bashing in a vehicle as rugged and tough as yourself.'

The intended audience here appears to be chiefly male. This text is aimed at the type of person who enjoys the outdoors and who likes to see themselves as tough and adventurous. The text does not exclude women with a taste for adventure.

5   'See you at the stadium on Saturday, my bra.'
    The audience here is probably an African soccer enthusiast and a friend of the speaker.

Activity 4 Purpose

1   'Have you heard the one about the Englishman, the Irishman and Van der Merwe?'
    This is clearly the opening line of a joke, so the purpose is to *entertain*.

2   'The code for all telephone numbers in the area has changed to 0132.'
    The purpose is to *inform*. The language is bare and factual. It imparts essential information only.

3   'Yesterday I had to wait for more than an hour for my train. This is unacceptable.'
    This is a *complaint*. The speaker is registering his or her dissatisfaction and obviously wants something done about the poor train service.

4   'Do have a doughnut – they are delicious. I got them fresh from the bakery this morning.'
    The purpose is to *persuade*. The speaker is doing more than offering a doughnut – he or she is trying to make them sound as tempting as possible.

5   'Open your textbooks at page 32. Do Exercise 15, making sure that you include the points we have been discussing.'
    The purpose is to *instruct*. The verbs are in the *imperative* form; the wording is precise and factual; and the instructions are arranged in sequence.

6   'If you buy one today, you could win the car of your dreams!'
    The purpose is to *sell* some unspecified commodity. An extra incentive is supplied by the offer of winning a car for a prize. Emotive language ('the car of your dreams') is used to *persuade*. The use of the word 'today' and an exclamation mark, add a sense of urgency.

7   The purpose of the cartoon is to *satirize*. Thus the cartoon has a double purpose. Firstly, it draws attention – in a humorous way – to the dreadful behaviour of human beings, and *amuses* the reader by presenting an ironic reversal of 'roles' of human beings and 'wild' animals (the lions are commenting on the humans' *savage* behaviour, instead of the other way round). Secondly, it *provokes* the reader into thinking about the serious issue of child rape.

Activity 5 Discourse analysis

Speaker/Writer	Context	Audience	Purpose
Unknown – no personal details are provided, but the writer must have cooking and writing skills to be able to produce this text.	Recipe book, or possibly the cookery section of a magazine or newspaper.	The general public, but more specifically those interested in new ways of preparing food, either as a hobby, or because they are obliged to cook for their families.	To *instruct*. All the verbs are in the imperative form; the steps in the cooking process are carefully stated in sequence; and only the necessary facts are given. The language is objective and factual.

Activity 6 Discourse analysis

Speaker/Writer	Context	Audience	Purpose
An advertiser employed by the management of the holiday resort. The persona assumed by the writer is professional rather than personal.	Probably an advertisement in a magazine or the travel section of a newspaper.	The general public, and potential holiday-makers, but only those affluent enough to afford such a holiday.	To *persuade*. This advertisement is designed to 'sell' this particular holiday resort, hence the use of emotive language: 'incredible beauty', and 'God's own creation'. Also to *inform*. Some facts and contact details are provided.

Activity 7 Discourse analysis

Speaker/Writer	Context	Audience	Purpose
Young male student (this information has been explicitly provided). We can infer from his remarks that he is non-assertive ('I don't think retaliation is the best remedy'). He is conscious of being physically smaller than those he would like to challenge, and this awareness makes him fear confrontation ('I'm afraid of fighting because I was born very thin'). He is obviously a conscientious student who is dedicated to earning his degree, when he refers to 'the bright future of hardworking students'.	Letter to the editor of a newspaper. This medium influences his choice of standard English in which to write this letter of complaint.	General public, but particularly those in charge at the Sammy Marks library, and those students who frequent the library and disturb others.	To *complain* about unacceptable noise levels, with the aim of *prompting action* to control the behaviour of certain inconsiderate students.

Bibliography

AKMAJIAN, Adrian *et al.* 1984. *Linguistics: An introduction to language and communication.* Cambridge, Massachusetts: The MIT Press.

ALEXANDER, N. 1989. *Language policy and national unity in South Africa/Azania*, pp. 12, 22, and 32. Cape Town: Buchu Books.

APPLEGATE, R. P. 1975. 'The language teacher and the rules of speaking' in the *TESOL Quarterly.* Vol. 9, No. 3, September, pp. 272–73.

BARBER, C. 1975. Adaptation of 'The later history of English', p. 330, in W. F. Bolton, ed. *The English language*, p. 330. London: Sphere Books.

BRANFORD, Jean. 1991. *A Dictionary of South African English.* Cape Town: Oxford University Press.

BRANFORD, William. 1996. Adaptation of 'English in South African society: a preliminary overview', in Vivian de Klerk, ed. *Focus on South Africa*, p. 36. Amsterdam: John Benjamins.

BROWN, Gillian, and George Yule. 1983. *Discourse analysis.* Cambridge: Cambridge University Press.

BROWNE, Chris. Hagar the Horrible (cartoon strips) from Press Features (Pty) Ltd, in *Pretoria News.* Johannesburg: The Independent Newspaper Group.

BUTLER, Guy. 1986. 'English in the new South Africa', *The English Academy Review* 3, (month unspecified), pp. 173–74.

CHISANGA, T. and KAMWANGA-MALU, N. M. 1997. 'Owning the other tongue: the English language in southern Africa' in *Multilingual and Multicultural Development*, Vol. 18, No 2.

COOK, V. 1991. *Second language learning and language teaching*, pp. 38–9, and 52–3. London: Edward Arnold.

CROWTHER, Jonathan, ed. 1995. *Oxford Advanced Learner's Dictionary of Current English.* Oxford: Oxford University Press.

CRYSTAL, David. 1987. *The Cambridge Encyclopedia of Language*, pp. 3, 97, 119, 358, 422, and Chapters 4 and 31. Cambridge: Cambridge University Press.

CRYSTAL, David. 1988. *The English language*, p. 24. Harmondsworth: Penguin Books.

CRYSTAL, David. 1994. 'Which English or English *which?*' in Mike Hayhoe and Stephen Parker, *Who owns English?* p. 113. Buckingham: Open University Press.

DHAMIJA, P. V. 1994. 'English as a multiform medium', in Mike Hayhoe and Stephen Parker, *Who owns English?* pp. 62 and 67. Buckingham: Open University Press.

DU PREEZ, H. 1997. *Meet the rainbow nation*, pp. 22 and 87. Pretoria: Kagiso Tertiary.

'English – the language of a new nation: The present-day linguistic situation of South Africa' (1998) in *Even more Englishes: studies 1996–1997*, p. 110. (Survey written by various contributors.) Amsterdam: John Benjamins.

FOX, Gwyneth, ed. 1994. *Essential English Dictionary.* London: Harper Collins Publishers.

HAYAKAWA, S. I. 1965. *Language in thought and action* (2nd edition) pp. 10, 12, and 14. London: George Allen and Unwin.

HEMINGWAY, E. *A farewell to arms*, p. 7. Harmondsworth: Penguin Books.

HEUGH, Kathleen, Amanda Siegruhn, and Peter Pluddemann, eds. 1995. *Multilingual education for South Africa.* Johannesburg: Heinemann.

KHUMALO, Joe. 1999. Article in *Pace Magazine*, June. Johannesburg: Caxton Publishers.

MAIL & GUARDIAN, July, August, and October, 1999. Johannesburg: The Independent Newspaper Group.

MCARTHUR, Tom. 1998. 'Guides to tomorrow's English' in *English Today*, 55, Vol. 14, No. 3, July, pp. 21–26.

MDA, Zakes. 1995. *Ways of dying*, p. 164. Cape Town: Oxford University Press.

MESTHRIE, Rajend, ed. 1995. *Language and social history. Studies in South African sociolinguistics.* Cape Town: David Philip.

MPHAHLELE, Es'kia. 1984. 'Prometheus in chains: The fate of English in South Africa' in *The English Academy Review* 2, November, p. 90.

MUNITICH, Brenda. 1992. *Thoko,* p. 1. Cape Town: Tafelberg.

NDEBELE, Njabulo. 1987. 'English and social change' in *The English Academy Review* 4, January, pp. 12–13.

NELSON MANDELA. 1994. *Long walk to freedom,* p. 322. Boston: Little, Brown.

NGUGI WA THIONG'O. 1986. *Decolonising the mind: the politics of language in African literature,* p. 16. London: James Curry.

PAN SOUTH AFRICAN LANGUAGE BOARD (PANSALB). Conference on 'Multilingualism in South African cities and towns: ideals and realities', 7–9 October 1999.

PICKFORD, John. 1995. 'Time to cheerfully split the infinitive', in *BBC worldwide,* p. 19, No. 33, July. Quoted in: 1998 Study Guide 1 for the Advanced Certificate in Education, p. 48, compiled by members of the ACE team. Pretoria: University of South Africa.

POTTER, A. 1987. *The context of literature written in English,* pp. 11–12. Cape Town: Maskew Miller Longman.

PRETORIA NEWS, 1999–2002. Johannesburg: The Independent Newspaper Group.

QUIRK, Randolf. 1993. 'Cultivate your lexicon if you know what I mean', 12 July. London: *The Times.*

ROODT, Christa. *See* PAN SOUTH AFRICAN.

ROWLING, J.K. *Harry Potter and the prisoner of Azkaban,* p. 7. London: Bloomsbury.

SEPAMLA, S. 1969. Da same, da same. *New Inscapes,* p. 280. R. Malan. Cape Town: Oxford University Press.

SHAKESPEARE, WILLIAM. *The Merchant of Venice,* III, i, 55–61. Oxford: Oxford University Press.

SILVA, Penny. 1996. *A Dictionary of South African English on Historical Principles.* Oxford: Oxford University Press.

SILVA, Penny. 1997. 'The lexis of South African English: reflections of a multilingual society' in *Englishes around the world* Vol 2, p. 160, ed. Schneider, Edgar W. Amsterdam: John Benjamins.

SMANGALISO, Mkhatshwa. 1999. 'Being multilingual defines being South African' in *Pansalb News,* April-June. Pretoria: Pan South African Language Board.

SOUTH AFRICA. 1996. The Constitution of the Republic of South Africa, Act 108, Section 6, No. 4. Cape Town and Pretoria: Government Printer.

South African Concise Oxford Dictionary. 2002. Cape Town: Oxford University Press.

SUNDAY TIMES, 1997–2001.

Johannesburg: The Independent Newspaper Group.

SWANN, Joan. 1992. *Girls, boys and language*. Oxford: Blackwell.

THOMAS, Linda and Wareing, Shan. 1999. *Language, society and power*, p. 87. London: Routledge.

TITLESTAD, Peter. 1998. 'South Africa's language ghosts' in *English Today 54*, Vol. 14, No. 2, April, pp. 33–39.

TRASK, R. L. 1995. *Language: the basics*, p. 174. London: Routledge.

YULE, George. 1995. *The study of language*. Cambridge Low Price Editions. Cambridge: Cambridge University Press.

WAINWRIGHT, Judith, and Jackie Hutton. 1992. *Your own words*, Chapter 5. Walton-on-Thames: Nelson.

ZAPIRO. Lion cartoon (untitled). *The Sunday Times*, November 11, 2001. Johannesburg: The Independent Newspaper Group.

Index